SLEEP & POTTY TRAINING

2 books in 1

The Ultimate Guide to Help You Get Through the Night and Get Rid of the Diaper

by **Carol Moore**

Disclaimer

All erudition contained in this book is given for informational and educational purposes only. The author is not in any way accountable for any results or outcomes that emanate from using this material. Constructive attempts have been made to provide information that is both accurate and effective, but the author is not bound for the accuracy or use/misuse of information.

Table of Contents

Baby Sleep Training
The Ultimate Solution Guide to Solve Child's Sleep Problems

Potty Training In 3 Days
A Step-By-Step Guide to Help Your Toddlers Go Free from Diapers

Baby
SLEEP
TRAINING

The Ultimate Solution Guide to Solve Child's Sleep Problems

by Carol Moore

Introduction

Becoming a parent is an incredibly beautiful and challenging experience at the same time.

Knowing how to manage a newborn and its sleep can become a turning point for both the parent and the child, it become possible with training and a lot of patience.

Sleep training is the process of helping a baby to learn to fall asleep at night. Although there are several methods of training a baby to sleep, no matter what method will be used, it is important to note that consistency and commitment are the two most important things in the process. This technique does not involve just helping the baby sleep, it also involves making the baby stay asleep all through the night.

Babies find it difficult to adjust between day and night and also, to fall asleep on their own.

Before you get desperate for nocturnal awakenings thinking that sleepless nights will never end, it is essential to have a couple of key principles on children's sleep.

The 'hope', for example, that a baby will sleep through the night is unrealistic because its biological clock works differently than that of an adult. As the child grows, his alternation of sleep and wakefulness also starts to develop. Reaching maturity even in sleep is a biological process.

In the first year of life, therefore, it is normal for a child to wake up often at night: it is essential to be aware that it is not a disorder (or whim!) but a completely physiological fact.

In the following chapter I will not immediately talk about the techniques to make the baby sleep since, to make it sleep peacefully, there are many other things that must be known and prepared. In fact, preparing the environment will be as important as the technique itself, perhaps even more so. The chances of your child having a long, restorative sleep will be very high.

Chapter One

Adapting to Your New Life

First Moments

*T*he term "newborn" refers to children and puppies of all animal species and indicates a period of time that varies according to the species but, in any case included, for mammals, within the weaning period. This period, in the child, corresponds to the first 28 days of life, beyond which it will become "suckling". Knowing the most important aspects concerning this short but intense period is essential.

During the first six weeks of your baby's life, parenting will be quite exhausting. Don't expect everything's peachy with your baby. Newborns do not follow common, pre-established standard behaviors, each one is different because they may sleep, feed, stay awake or doze off in a completely different way than another. Babies tend to sleep a lot (almost all the time) but not for long and they breastfeed every three hours, so be ready as you'll need to be on duty 24/7 (they often wake up just when you just fell asleep!)

Despite a mom having been pregnant for nine months, this creature will be a new person to get to know through and through. Just like any person you may know, there will be new evolutions in your relationship that will allow you to build a solid relationship. Getting to know your baby requires patience and a little time!

Below are some of the characteristics that distinguish our babies.

Skin

The baby's skin may gradually become reddish and dry, in some cases even bluish. There is no need to worry since this is the result of the effort of childbirth. The skin can also be covered with spots that will disappear within a few days. It is also normal that children who are born after the term can have very dry and cracked skin. Also, all newborns have a decrease in weight which is due to the loss of fluids that are not compensated by food intake (few fluids ingested). It is usually less than 10% and does not require any action.

If the baby turns yellow, it means he has so-called neonatal jaundice. What does it mean? Babies in the mother's womb need more red blood cells, contained in the blood, than when they begin extrauterine life. For this reason, after birth it can happen that the red blood cells in excess "break": this leads to the accumulation of a substance called bilirubin that colors the skin yellow. The liver, which is not yet mature, cannot dispose of it and for this reason the skin takes on a yellowish color. This value is kept under control in the first 3 days of life through a simple test: if it exceeds a certain value, neonatologists appropriately intervene with phototherapy which is a very effective method to reduce bilirubin and absolutely non-invasive.

Fontanels

The name fontanel derives from the fact that, at times, it is possible to hear them pulsing, like a small fountain. They are made of soft and fibrous, but very strong tissue, and are located between the various bones of the skull. The fontanelles are important because they provide the baby's head with the elasticity that allows it to pass through the birth canal, and gradually disappear once the head expands and develops. Furthermore, the fontanelles allow the rapid growth of the skull, which occurs in particular in the first year of life.

In total, the fontanels are six, but in reality, only two, the anterior one (larger) and the posterior one (smaller) are of significant size, the others are very small and hardly palpable.

For the presence of certain medical conditions, the fontanels can change, resulting protruding, wider or narrower than normal, or deeper (or sunken).

The main fontanels close around the year of life, with some individual variables. Usually, however, at 18 months the main one should be closed. The garment should be gently caressed, but there are no particular risks or dangers.

Hearing

Hearing is the infant's first sense to develop.

For this reason, babies tend to be particularly sensitive to loud noises. Babies begin to refine their sense of hearing already in the uterus, especially during the third trimester, when studies establish that they can hear the heartbeat of mothers and capture some external sounds such as voices or music. Newborns' sense of hearing develops completely at the end of the first month of life, although it is clear that they do not understand exactly what they are hearing.

Feeding Time

In the first months of life, the baby should eat at least 8 meals a day (approximately every 3 hours).

Many breastfeeding mothers prefer, however, to opt for on-demand breastfeeding, latching the baby to the breast whenever the baby expresses the need to eat. There is no rule. Neither right nor wrong behavior. If the baby grows smoothly, any choice is correct.

Once in the mother's lap, the baby can be attached to the breast. Keep in mind that in the first half hour of life the newborn is generally very active, after which a physiological phase of relaxation follows after the stress of childbirth, in which it is normal for it to fall asleep. This is why the 20-30 minutes after birth are the ideal ones in which to start breastfeeding, to immediately stimulate milk production and promote the mother-baby bond.

It is normal for mothers (especially first-time mothers) to have no milk in the first days after giving birth. Milk whipping usually occurs 2-3 days after birth, sometimes even 4-5 days in mothers with their first child. In the meantime, the newborn should be attached to the breast every time she feels the need (in any case every 2 hours) because she is satisfied by the colostrum which is the first product of the mammary gland, rich in proteins, mineral salts, vitamins and factors that stimulate the immune system, promotes the maturation of the intestine and prepares it to receive mature milk. The important thing is that the diet is exclusively based on milk (for bottle-fed babies the milk must be the formulated one) and, at most, water.

During each feeding, the baby should consume between 18 fl oz and 22 fl oz of milk. Massage of the breasts, stretching and rotation of the nipple are essential to facilitate the production and ejection of milk, to reduce swelling and engorgement. Normally these maneuvers, as well as the position to be taken during breastfeeding and the way to support the breast and offer the nipple to facilitate sucking, are illustrated by the staff (midwives and nurses who help in the care of the newborn). At the end of the feeding it is good to help the baby to burp by holding it for a few minutes in a vertical position with the head resting on the shoulder (if it does not do so, don't worry!).

It is necessary to treat very well the attack of the child to the breast. A suitable attack, in which the child's mouth not only grabs the nipple, but also a good part of the areola, with the chin sinking into the breast, ensures an effective suction and therefore a good production of milk and reduces the risk of developing rhagades.

Infant Reflux

Regurgitating small amounts of milk after feeding is very common among infants, starting from the first weeks of life. However, there is great individual variability: some babies regurgitate very often, while others do it infrequently. It appears from the first milk intake and tends to disappear around 12, maximum 18 months of life. So, it can also happen during weaning with the first baby food. There are three types of reflux in infants:

− physiological: in this case it is not worrying for his health

− chronic: with visible decline in growth, on this occasion the mother should contact the pediatrician to understand the cause and find remedies for the problem.

— symptomatic: if it occurs often, even if the child grows normally and her weight does not fluctuate considerably.

In the first year of life, the cause of this annoying phenomenon comes from the digestive system, which is not yet used to working in that way to feed the baby's body.

To control regurgitation, it is advisable to hold the baby in your arms, preferably in a vertical position, for about 15 minutes after the end of the feed. This helps on the one hand to avoid that the famous burp resulting from regurgitation is hard to be emitted, on the other hand to avoid the risk of milk rising from the stomach to the mouth when the baby is lying down. If it is lying on the bed, it will need to be placed with the head raised by 30 degrees, so that the milk can remain in the stomach for digestion and the valve can perform its normal work. When placed in the cradle it must be placed on the back because if a regurgitation should arrive the baby will automatically tend to turn her head to one side and let the liquid out.

Even the introduction of solid foods in the child's diet favors the disappearance of the phenomenon, which is accentuated in the presence of excessive liquids.

Crying

The child, in the first months of life, unable to communicate directly, draws the parents' attention with crying. She cries for different reasons: need for protection, comfort and contact, hunger, cold or hot, discomfort, for example from getting wet or dirty, ache, too much noise, something scaring, sense of loneliness, expression of emotions. In fact, from the first days of life, the primary emotions of the human being are present, that is joy, sadness, anger, fear, disgust and surprise, which can manifest themselves, perhaps in a somewhat confused way, through tears. Crying was the communication tool that the child selected for its survival, if it did not cry, in fact, one would think that everything is going for the best.

In short, crying is the tool to say everything and it is very important that mum and dad quickly learn to recognize the different forms of crying in order to respond promptly to the needs of the little one.

Crying is always a request for help or, more generally, for communication, which must be accepted without hesitation. The idea that running when the baby cries is equivalent to making him grow up "spoiled" is a legacy of a distant time marked by a harmful indifference towards the emotional well-being of newborns.

At Home

"It will turn your life upside down": how many times does a pregnant woman hear it? And, unlike many other considerations that are addressed to a future mother, it is just like that. A newborn baby needs constant, practical - changing diapers, bathing, clothes, more changing diapers -

and emotional care. And as much as a parent feels prepared for the task ahead, surprises are not long in coming. However, as the days go by you will become expert and very practical, experience is everything. But also trust your instincts, in most cases it is right.

FIVE IMPORTANT RULES

Sleep if the baby is sleeping too

When the baby is resting, the mother should do it too rather than devote herself to the house or do anything else.

You can choose a classic cradle to be placed more or less close to the bed, or a bedside cradle, as a place to let it sleep, especially recommended if the mother is breastfeeding and wants to do it as long as possible, since breastfeeding should take place "on demand" and in the first weeks it tends to be quite frequent even at night.

The so-called co-sleeping, or making the newborn sleep in the bed, is a very practical choice especially for the nursing mother. The newborn next to the parent tends to sleep longer because she is in a more protected environment and partly similar to that of the uterus (he can hear the sound of the mother's heart, its smell and its heat). Even if she wakes up because her limbs are suddenly moving (moor reflex), she can fall asleep more easily.

When deciding where to sleep, it is also important to make sure that the environment is suitable for a good rest. In particular, the temperature of the room where the newborn sleeps must be between 68 ° F and 72 ° F. Babies suffer a lot from both heat and cold so it is important that the temperature is kept constant. The humidity rate, around 50%, is also important to facilitate the baby's breathing.

It is important that parents do their best to accustom the child to moments of light and dark, making her sleep during the day with the light and in the dark at night both to get her used to distinguishing day from night, and because the child benefits from exposure to natural light.

Finally, wherever the baby sleeps, the mattress must be rigid, without spaces or gaps in which the baby could get stuck. The pillow must not be used and there must be no objects in the cradle that could limit the baby's breathing (for example puppets, soft toys, pillows, wrinkled sheets), at least up to 3/6 months of life. No duvets or too abundant blankets. Pay attention to the fact that (light) blankets should never cover the baby's head; if the parents are cold, they can wear heavier pajamas or sweaters. No siblings or pets on the bed and the baby should be at the side of the bed towards the mother (not in the middle) where a special protection must be mounted to prevent the baby from falling.

Avoid visits

When you come home after giving birth with the baby everyone wants to come and see you. And although relatives, friends and colleagues are animated by a genuine feeling of kindness, you should limit visits. Set times and days, and when they arrive, don't be ashamed to be found in overalls or pajamas, or tell them to leave if you and the baby start feeling tired. It should be avoided that visitors arrive at any time of the day and that they hold the baby in their arms for a long time.

Too intense scents should be avoided as well as the smell of smoke that will surely annoy the baby.

It is a good rule for those who approach the newborn to wash their hands with soap and water; if this is not possible, it is preferable to ask people to avoid picking her up in order not to put her health at too much risk. It goes without saying that kissing a baby for a few hours or days is absolutely forbidden, even when it comes to close relatives, let alone in the case of strangers. So, ask the people who visit you to refrain from this type of effusions that could transmit germs and bacteria to the defenseless child.

Get help by taking breaks

Ask for help with shopping, for housework, call a friend who is watching the baby while you take a shower in peace. If you see that you can't make it, and grandparents or relatives live far away, or you just don't want family meddling, consider hiring a specialized babysitter. Also, try to find some moments for yourself, a coffee with a friend, hairdresser, take a ride.

Eat well and drink lots of water

It is certainly not the time for diets after childbirth, but great care must be taken to choose the correct foods and make the right combinations, to quickly recover energy, and good mood. Get help with cooking if possible and eat healthily while drinking plenty of water. Having spent a sleepless night, between feedings and diaper changes, you will need to have a hearty breakfast that will give you that energy to face the day. Make sure you maintain a balanced diet with micro and macro nutrients, foods from which you can find sources of calcium and magnesium and foods rich in Omega3. Eat early in the evening so that food does not interfere with the few hours of sleep you have available and try to overeat. Don't forget to drink a lot as you will need more water when breastfeeding. Also, try to avoid sugar and its derivatives, alcohol, coffee, tea and cola-based drinks.

Share with your partner

Of course, the birth of the baby is not just your "business". You will share tasks and problems but also many joys. This will be very good for the couple, as you will have a new and fascinating common reality to support one another.

While moms obviously play the most important role in breastfeeding, there are many things your partner and other family members can do to support and bond with the baby, such as helping to settle and calm him with skin contact. leather or carry it in a headband.

They will be able to help you keep an eye on her while you rest even for a few tens of minutes.

TRAVELING WITH THE NEWBORN

Infants, contrary to popular belief, can face any type of journey, as long as the conditions necessary for their comfort are present. Assuming you take it to places that are healthy and do not need vaccination prophylaxis, your baby can come anywhere if her is in good health. They can also travel by plane, in fact, after the first month there is no contraindication. If babies are breastfed, everything is easier, fewer things to pack, but even those who are undergoing artificial feeding will not have major difficulties, there are very light sterilizers to carry in your suitcase.

We must, however, be careful as, for the first three months, the newborn begins a period of adaptation to life extra-uterine. Even new parents must learn to know the baby and to adapt to new rhythms. All in all, I would recommend starting to travel after the first 2/3 months excluding of course, very extreme destinations (very hot or very cold places).

In fact, at three months, your baby will presumably have established a sleep-baby-change routine, and her will be strong enough to deal with a new environment and new conditions. If you enjoy traveling, take advantage of the fact that airlines do not charge children up to the age of two (as long as they don't take a seat). Among other things, traveling by plane with a newborn is much easier and more relaxing than traveling with a two or five years-old child.

In infants, traveling has a sleep-inducing effect.

In many infants it can be observed that not only the cradle, but also many other forms of rhythmic stimuli, such as traveling in a train or car, have a sleep-inducing effect.

Some experiments carried out by experts in pediatrics and child medicine have shown that infants prefer rhythmic sounds to total silence. Science seeks to understand whether the rhythmic heartbeat of the mother, known to the newborn from pregnancy, or even the sounds of the parents' breathing have to do with this preference of babies. In fact, some newborns seem to "lull" themselves into sleep through rhythmic movements of the legs or head.

TAKE THE BABY OUTDOOR

You should go out with your baby right away, go out in the open air, in fact, it will be good for both new parents and newborn. If you are planning a short walk in the open air, and your baby does not exceed 13 or 15 pounds, the baby carrier is very suitable: the heat and contact with your body will favor the tranquility of the little one who will almost certainly take a nice nap. The backyard garden is the perfect place for mothers who, especially in the early days, may not feel like making long journeys or simply need a bench where they can stop, for example, to breastfeed their child.

Newborn babies generally eat every two to three hours. If the mother is breastfeeding, especially in spring and summer, there is no problem. In fact, at any time, she can stop and feed her baby. For the others it is necessary to organize themselves with the feedings. If necessary, it is possible to bring with you a bottle and a package of liquid milk to be heated in the microwave or, in a thermos, the amount of hot water required and the equivalent of powdered milk)

Apart from these small tricks, there are no limits to the duration of the walk. If the weather is mild, the weather conditions are good and it is not too cold, mum and dad can be around with their baby for as long as they want. Long walks are not recommended when there is excessive cold or too much wind (the dust raised, in fact, can cause irritation to the child or facilitate the spread of various infections). Rush hours are also to be avoided, when the traffic is more intense and the air, especially in big cities, is more polluted and particularly crowded areas. In the very first days of life, it is also good to avoid public places with a high density of attendance (shopping malls, department stores, markets ...) where the possibility of contracting viruses and infections is greater.

Choose routes away from car traffic and not crowded since children are the most exposed to the damage caused by environmental pollution. Do not park the wheelchair on the pavement near a traffic light due to the higher amount of exhaust gases and remember to get off the curb first and then let the wheelchair out.

Winter

In winter it is important that the child is well covered (scarf, hat and gloves are fine) but it will be necessary to relieve her of clothing every time he enters a shop or a heated place. The walk with babies in winter should be done at slightly warmer times, so in the late morning or early afternoon. Cover the baby well, but do not suffocate her under duvets, blankets and scarves. If the temperatures are very low or there is a risk of rain, you can use the transparent wax that practically all strollers are supplied with, but it would be better to let them breathe freely. If your newborn's skin is particularly delicate (and this is the case for most babies), before leaving them in winter cold, it is advisable to use a light moisturizer, and spread it in particular on the face, so that it does not become reddish.

Summer

First of all, for the morning walk, you can choose to go out very early, otherwise for the evening walk. In this way, you will avoid the hottest hours, i.e. from 11:00 to 17:00, hours when children should not be exposed to the sun. Prefer shady places, such as parks surrounded by nature and trees, thus avoiding the strong heat emanating from the concrete of the asphalt.

When walking in the sun, be careful to protect the baby with cotton caps and fresh clothes, as well as with protective sunscreen, as the rays filter and reach the baby's skin, even if you are not on the beach. Don't be too apprehensive, covering the little one too much; do not fear even a little wind by the sea. Try to think that your child does not feel colder or less warm than parents and consequently you will have to dress them exactly as you do, if not less because babies and very young children can sweat a lot.

If you are breastfeeding exclusively, offer the chest on request and even more frequently on the hottest days.

In summer, however, it should not be exposed to direct sunlight but normal exposure to sunlight promotes the absorption of vitamin D, which is essential for the assimilation of calcium, therefore for the health of bones and teeth. Even if we are in February, always remember to put a mosquito net on the pram, so that any direct rays reach your child in a more attenuated way.

Survival Kit

When going out with a baby you should never leave home:

- Three or four nappies for changing, a towel to place on public changing tables, wet wipes and a cream for the buttocks

- a spare leotard and a onesie in case the baby gets dirty (in the first weeks, when the baby's feeding is exclusively liquid this can happen)

- a blanket or a sheet, depending on the season, to keep in the stroller basket

- a small rain cover and, in the summer season, mosquito net for stroller

- a pacifier if used by the child

- sanitizing wipes.

BABY BATH

The first baby bath is a moment of great emotion for mothers, who, often overwhelmed by anxiety and the worry of doing something wrong, experience this moment with great embarrassment. In the first months of life, however, this moment represents a further opportunity for exchange and interaction between mother and child, in the form of cuddles, contacts, games, cries and laughter as well as stimulating the senses of smell and touch, awakening the attention and familiarity with water. Even if there is no objective need to bathe the baby every day, we advise you to adopt this good habit that will also favor the little one's sleep. If you should notice that your child experiences the bath as a moment of tension or discomfort, it will be better not to do it every day, but to reduce the frequency, alternating it with simple sponging.

The baby's first bath should take place the day after birth (24 hours); it is not necessary to wait for the umbilical stump to be detached, it is only important to dry it well and wrap it with a piece of gauze to help it drying. The duration of the baby's bath should not exceed 10-15 minutes.

Remember, at this age, baby's skin is still very fragile and delicate so to avoid redness and not compromise the natural skin barrier, we recommend using specific products for babies, non-aggressive, non-foaming or perfumed products, which could irritate and dry the skin. There is no need for sponges or washcloths, just mum's clean hand is enough. In the long run, sponges can be a concentrate of bacteria. Better to do it only with water or with mild oily cleansers. A natural alternative to make baby's skin soft: a drop of milk or a spoonful of olive oil in water.

Set-up

Before bathing the baby, it is important to prepare everything you need: everything must be close at hand because during the bath the baby must never be left alone.

In general, it is good to wait at least two hours after feeding, to be sure that the baby has digested well: during the bath, in fact, the baby could get cold and run into congestion. Done in the evening, it can be a great way to help your baby sleep.

In particular, the material that will be used and that must be at hand for the baby's bath includes:

- delicate detergent specific for children, with neutral pH

- thermometer

- gauzes and wadding for cleaning the face

- moisturizers and zinc oxide product

- soft terry towel

- clean clothes (body and onesie) and diaper

- tray with a cushion or rubber mat on the bottom to reduce slipping and to support the baby.

It is also necessary to ensure that:

- the environment has a temperature between 68 ° and 72°, which is very important to prevent the baby from getting cold both before and after the bath. If the room temperature is lower, it should be warmed up. It is also important that there are no large changes in temperature between one room and another, so as to avoid any cooling

- there are no direct lights that are too strong, especially if it is evening it is better to favor a relaxed atmosphere with semi-soft lights

- the water in the tub has a temperature between 97-100°; in practice, the temperature must be similar to that of the human body

— you do not have any jewelry or rings that could accidentally scratch the skin of the child.

After these preliminary actions you can start with the actual bath:

Undress the baby by placing it supine on a support base, paying particular attention to the head, which is difficult for the baby to control. Also remove the diaper as the last thing.

Immerse the baby up to shoulder height slowly, so that she feels completely warm and can experience the pleasant sensation she experienced for nine months in amniotic fluid again, maintaining a firm and secure grip. During the bath, the head and torso must be supported with the forearm; the left hand goes into the baby's axilla, so that she can be washed with the right hand.

Start washing the baby always starting from the upper part of the body, from the neck, then going towards the genitals, or always start from the "clean" area to the dirty one. During washing, particular attention must be paid to skin folds (neck, retro-auricular area, armpits, interdigital spaces, groin), hands, feet and nails. Facial cleansing must be performed separately, avoiding the penetration of water into the eyes, nose and ears.

If supporting the baby in the water seems difficult, you can lather it on the changing table and rinse it in the water later.

To cheer up the baby it would be great to continue communicating with her, explaining what to do. It may seem absurd at such an age, but they already understand a lot and doing something without their "agreement" can cause the worst ire.

When the time comes to let the baby out of the water, grab her with a firm and secure grip under the armpits and immediately wrap her in a soft towel before placing her on the changing table (this operation must be performed as quickly as possible to prevent the newborn takes cold); dry her by gently patting the skin, without rubbing, to avoid skin lesions (it is recommended to use linen towels).

Always pay attention to skin folds, these areas must be dried well because water residues could macerate the skin. During this phase, dry the entire area surrounding the umbilical cord thoroughly.

Gently distribute the cream or moisturizing oil by massaging the baby's skin; avoiding using talcum powder as it could be dangerous if inhaled by the baby. The important thing is to well dry the part of the cord attached to the navel and medicate it as the hospital staff will show you immediately after the childbirth. Dress the baby and comb her. At the end of the bath it is good practice to always clean and disinfect the tub.

The only complications of the bath are represented by hypothermia, hyperthermia and burns therefore, the evaluation of the temperature is fundamental.

Although it is customary, after bathing the newborn, the use of talcum powder should be avoided as it could be inhaled by the child, especially when used in large doses on the chest and upper limbs.

Further advice

The ears should be cleaned several times a week, with a stick covered with cotton wool, but only externally, at the level of the auricle, in fact it is necessary to clean only the areas that can be seen, avoiding penetrating too deeply into the auditory canal or in the nose of the newborn. Given the fragility of the newborn, an injury to the eardrum membrane could be accidentally caused.

The toenails should be cut a couple of times a month with a straight, rounded-tip scissors to prevent ingrowning, the corners of the scissors for the fingers must also be rounded in order to prevent any scratches. If your baby is not standing still, it is advisable to do this while sleeping.

Every day it would be great to use a soft and long bristle brush to free the scalp from any traces of dandruff.

Talc can create a barrier that prevents the skin from breathing.

Perfect Baby Room Set-Up

Most parents know it because they have been through it and would not wish it even on the worst enemy: when a newborn does not sleep, the tranquility of the whole family is undermined and, if the sleepless nights can appear long, the days without having rested are definitely interminable. So, let's see what are the things that must be present in the baby's room to promote a peaceful sleep, as long as possible.

THE LAYETTE

The Mattress

Before talking about the routines and techniques for the baby to fall asleep, it is necessary to analyze the preparation aspects of the place where the baby will sleep. First of all, we must mention the mattress, an important but often underestimated element, which, if made of good quality, will give your child a better sleep, to the delight of the whole family!

The correct density of the mattress must be neither too high nor too low. In fact, if it is too hard, the mattress can harm the baby's comfort and cause the flat head syndrome. If the density is too low, on the other hand, there is a risk of the mattress collapsing and loss of balance when the child is sitting.

It would be better not to reuse the brothers' mattress. Think, in fact, of the dust, sweat, vomiting or pee that sooner or later end up on their beds, becoming fertile ground for the proliferation of mites and bacteria.

Furthermore, the structural part of the mattress must also be well ventilated because during sleep the baby loses on average, by sweating, a lot of water which evaporating passes into the internal layers of the mattress, where it creates, if not removed with the air circulation, an environment wet suitable for the proliferation of bacteria and molds. Nobody will do it every day as the guidelines say but try to turn it at least once every two weeks, especially if it rests on a closed surface and therefore has a reduced ventilation cycle. Even if made of latex, turn it often, as it is the material that more than any other causes allergies.

There is a special material for children who suffer from allergies to dust mites, it is called "x-static" and, thanks to the silver fibers contained within it, it prevents the proliferation of bacteria, which the mites feed on. This means that almost all of the mites will disappear and sleep will be more peaceful for those suffering from this allergy.

I think that the optimal solution for the newborn is a fiber mattress with a small layer of "Memory", since being able to alternate them, it is possible to use the memory side, which tends to be a little warmer, during the winter and the fiber for the summer one.

The Baby Sheet

Before purchasing a sheet for the baby's crib, it is necessary to pay adequate attention to the dimensions, i.e. the width and length, which must adapt perfectly to the mattress of the cradle in which the baby will sleep. For her safety it is essential that the sheet is neither too small nor too abundant, because the folds of the fabric could cause serious accidents.

The material for making the sheets must be a natural, breathable, hypoallergenic and soft yarn. Cotton is the ideal fabric, since it meets all the requirements described, in fact, the very delicate skin of the newborn baby is subject to multiple external attacks and her immune system is not yet developing, so the natural cotton sheet is the best choice.

We also recommend that you iron the sheet after washing and before use, to make it even softer.

Blanket

As for the baby blanket to put in the layette, the first things to pay attention to should not be the design, style or colors, but the comfort and quality of the fabrics.

In fact, the baby, with its skin so delicate, needs the utmost delicacy and care and being so small, it needs light, soft and breathable fabrics that guarantee a peaceful sleep.

Cotton (if 100%) is a soft natural fabric that does not irritate the delicate skin of babies. Since it is breathable, it allows better air circulation and, being absorbent, it helps to remove and absorb body moisture, keeping the body cool and dry. For these reasons, it guarantees the child an ideal environment to sleep peacefully and without discomfort. It is also very practical, has a high tensile strength and, even withstanding high washing temperatures, can be sterilized. And importantly, it is always suitable at any time of the year. On the market, however, there are also cotton blend covers, i.e. cotton with the addition of innovative synthetic materials.

Wool is one of the oldest natural fibers of animal origin. It is certainly soft and warm and, thanks to its ability to retain a greater amount of air, it is very insulating from both cold and heat. It easily absorbs water and sweat more than cotton, without giving the impression of being damp. The wool covers also have a good resistance to wear, crease very little and are quite elastic so they can be stretched and widened without breaking and then returned to their original size.

A flaw with the wool blanket, however, is that it needs more attention than a cotton one. In fact, washes must be done at low temperatures and with detergents for delicate products, otherwise they will become felted. In addition, wool tends to yellow over time and, not least, can cause irritation.

Finally, fleece is a "fabric" particularly appreciated for its numerous qualities even if it is not natural but synthetic.

Thanks to a particular processing of polyester fibers (PET), the fleece is very soft, velvety and pleasant to the touch. Furthermore, the fiber processed in this way contains a lot of air and this allows the fleece to be a good thermal insulator.

Pillow

The pillow, as we know in the first months of the baby is not essential. However, if the baby is suffering from regurgitation, it can be a big hand to keep the problem at bay. In fact, small inclined pillows are marketed to help contain the consequences of refluxes.

SCREENS

All screens (TV, tablets, phones, and computer) should be turned off thirty minutes before sleep time. It had been observed that screen light just before sleeping time affects the ability of the baby to sleep well.

LIGHTS

When a baby is born, it becomes practically obligatory for parents to think about how to illuminate the room where the child sleeps during the night (which is often that of mom and dad). It is not so much to prevent the fear of the dark, which occurs around 2 years of age, but rather to give a useful reference point for your baby, to manage the awakenings (more or less numerous) during the night.

It is good that the night light for children is not a normal bedside lamp: if the child sees an intense light, in fact, she can be led to think that it is not the time to sleep, and therefore wake up or struggle to resume sleep.

As a night light, we should choose low intensity lamps (maximum 7 watts), which do not overheat too much during use to avoid getting burned, and which offer good energy savings.

It is better to use LED lamps since they produce much less heat than incandescent bulbs. This makes LEDs safer and also more energy efficient and moreover, they also last much longer than other bulbs commonly used in night lights. There are conflicting opinions on choosing the color, and it is easy to come across the advice to prefer colors such as blue or green because they are "soothing".

In fact, a Harvard University study has refuted this thesis by showing that blue light reduces the production of melatonin by 99%, the hormone that regulates the sleep-wake cycle in humans.

However, given that the presence of a minimum luminous "trace" is practically essential for new parents, especially in the first months of the child's life (ie when the child, on average, still has to learn to manage the moments of wakefulness and those of sleep), the advice is to prefer lights that have a longer wavelength, such as red or amber-colored ones, because they have no effect on melatonin production.

It will also be possible to use socket night lights, socket lights with applique (to be mounted on the wall, drilling it), or portable lights.

The former has the advantage of being able to be transferred from one outlet to another, depending on convenience, while the latter are those that generally manage to furnish more than the others, but it must be taken into account that the choice is not reversible.

Precisely, for this last reason, many prefer to focus on portable night lights, which can be moved where you want easily even several times during the day and night, and do not have the limit of having to be connected to a power outlet except for recharging the battery.

You can also try a pink salt lamp; leave a Himalayan pink salt lamp on in the room for as many hours as possible, even during the night if necessary, especially for children who are afraid of the dark.

When heated, the lamp will release negative ions that will improve air quality by reducing electromagnetic pollution, often the cause of disturbed sleep.

ESSENTIAL OILS

To promote the baby's sleep, it is possible to use essential oils. Due to their high concentration, the use of these oils is usually not recommended in infants, however, if topical use is to be discouraged on children under six months, their diffusion in environments has no contraindications. To best benefit from the properties of the essences, it is important to choose them of excellent quality, avoiding dilutions with addition of synthetic substances, as they could cause skin and health problems in general. These volatile oils extracted from plants have the ability to influence mood, emotions and are often used to for aromatic baths, for massages or to perfume the environment.

For this purpose, the most suitable oils are: true lavender (Lavandula angustifolia) which has relaxing properties for the day, but especially for the night; Roman chamomile (Anthemis nobilis), particularly if, at the time of sleep, the child tends to become nervous and irritable; mandarin (citrus reticulata), par excellence the children's oil.

It is possible to put 1/2 drops of lavender oil in the essence diffuser (avoid the "essence burner" candle ones, as by heating the oils, toxic substances are dispersed into the environment).

Alternatively, a few drops of lavender essential oil on a pillow, to be left near the baby, or on its favorite soft toy.

Or, depending on the room, you can place a basin of water on a lit heater and dilute 5-6 drops of essential oil in water.

If the baby is older than six months, you can also use one or two drops of essential oil in the bath. In this case it is essential to dilute them in a teaspoon of milk or cream as the essential oils are not water-soluble.

BACH FLOWERS

Another totally harmless natural remedy to promote the baby's sleep are Bach flowers. These floral infusions have no contraindications and can be safely administered even in early childhood. Based on the sleep disorder type, it is possible to identify some flowers suitable for that particular situation.

If the child has mistaken the day for the night, the Scleranthus flower will be needed; if her falls asleep only in her mother's arms and requires continuous attention, the Chicory/Heather combination will have to be used; if it is excessive tiredness that prevents it from falling asleep the right flower will be Olive; Walnut helps the child to adapt to sleep-wake rhythms; Vervain to limit the over-stimulus crying; Cherry Plum (flower of control) helps the little one to rely and let go when she has to fall asleep; Aspen helps to better manage anxiety and baseless fears (when you are afraid but you don't know what).

At the herbalist's shop they will prepare the mixture of flowers that you will indicate.

SCHÜSSLER SALTS

Schlusser salts or tissue salts are twelve preparations based on diluted mineral salts, used for therapeutic purposes in natural and complementary medicine, designed in the second half of the nineteenth century by the German doctor Wilhelm Schüssler. Dr. Schüssler stated that cells make tissues sick when they no longer contain minerals in the correct amount that they need to maintain good health.

Among the twelve salts discovered by Dr. Schüssler, Magnesium Phosphoricum is certainly suitable for promoting relaxation of the body and mind. In fact, Magnesium Phosphoricum is recommended for insomnia, abdominal colic also caused by states of agitation, in the presence of cough and when the child is particularly "hyperactive", obviously not excluding some dietary precautions during daily meals. This salt regulates the sleep-wake rhythm, favoring falling asleep but also the morning awakening with more vitality.

For the dosage it is advisable to refer to the manufacturer based on the age of the child.

WHITE NOISE

You know the white light, the one that represents the sum of all visible colors? Well, in the same way, white noise is practically the sum of all audible frequencies and sounds such as those of the hair dryer, vacuum cleaner, hood or fan that come very close to it.

Precisely because it is the sum of other frequencies, white noise helps to mask individual sounds that could be annoying, such as those of traffic or people talking in a neighboring room. White noise basically accompanies newborns in Morpheus' arms in a natural and progressive way. However, we must not think that white noise is something purely artificial, because even in nature it is possible to find white noise: think, for example, of the sound of pouring or constant rain, of mountain waterfalls or of a flowing river.

On the net there are audio files and playlists that reproduce the so-called white noise or devices that reproduce relaxing sounds such as that of the undertow or a forest. Alternatively, you can try do-it-yourself solutions such as turning on the vacuum cleaner or hairdryer while trying to put the baby to sleep. A variant of the white noise method, sometimes also used with puppies of other mammals, consists in making the newborn listen to a sound that reminds them of the beating of the mother's heart, for example using an alarm clock or a special recording.

Be careful not to use it for too long, always keep the volume down and place the device away from the child. I recommend not to exaggerate, it is okay if you are using a background sound of this type for a few minutes, but it is not the case to keep the noise source on all night. Otherwise, the risk is that it becomes a nuisance and interfere with the baby's sleep quality.

Chapter Two

What to Know About Baby Sleep

I t happens a bit to everyone to look at this little man or little woman and have almost a little fear of it. In fact, they often communicate things we do not understand, such as crying. The most important thing, however, is to know as much as possible so as to suffer much less the negative effects that can derive from growing the baby.

Physiology of Baby Sleep

Thinking that a child's sleep is similar to that of an adult is a very widespread idea but, at the same time, it is wrong. In fact, sleep is a complex phenomenon, which evolves and changes during growth. In the first months of life we spend about 70-80% of the time sleeping: the hours of sleep for the newborn are about 15-20 hours a day, while for seniors, they reach 5-6 hours. As the baby grows, however, there is still more similarity with the adult sleep.

In general, babies and children sleep more mainly because sleep affects their growth, in particular by promoting brain development (especially the REM phase sleep, i.e. the lightest one), consolidating memory and everything that the child learns during day, stimulating the secretion of growth hormone, strengthening the immune system and allowing the body to slow down and the brain to "cleanse itself" of toxins accumulated during wakefulness.

The infant's sleep is dominated by instinctive motivations, by primary impulses such as hunger or thirst. The need to take small and frequent meals, resulting from poor gastric capacity and imposing growth rates, causes the baby's biological rhythm to oscillate around 3-4 hours, and is well connected to the hunger-satiety cycle. Bottle-fed babies generally tend to sleep for longer periods than breastfed babies, which may require frequent feedings, up to 12 per day.

Sleep also evolves throughout the day and is divided into cycles, lasting about an hour (90-120 minutes for older children and adults). Even during the night, the cycles follow one after the other; it is therefore wrong to think that sleep (of the newborn as well as of the adult) is continuous. Furthermore, within the single cycle (this also applies to both children and adults) there are "phases" that are different from each other in terms of amount of time.

REM and non-REM Phase

Acronym for Rapid Eye Movement (rapid eye movements), REM is a phase of light sleep, studded with dreams and characterized by phasic movements of the limbs, face and body, with irregular breathing and heart rate. The small movements of the face or the appearance of facial expressions of fear, surprise, joy and big smiles, are signs of brain activity linked to the learning of emotions and the ability to communicate them. There may also be sudden jolts. During sleep, the newborn is in this REM phase for about 50% of the time, while in older children REM sleep is more contained (it drops to 15% in adults).

Non-REM sleep consists of four stages: sleepiness (1), light sleep (2), deep sleep (3) and very deep sleep (4). When a newborn is ready to fall asleep, it goes through these four stages in progression, after which it takes the reverse path up to point two and enters the REM sleep stage (1 - 2 - 3 - 4 - 3 -2 - REM). This cycle is repeated several times during rest and implies a certain ease upon awakening in the transition from deep sleep to light sleep.

The 60 minutes that make up a baby's sleep cycle are split between REM and non-REM. At birth, REM sleep represents about 50% of the total, around 2-3 years it becomes 25%, to then reach (as in adults) about 20% around 6 years. As anticipated, the percentage of REM sleep in children is higher because it is functional to brain development.

Recent studies seem to indicate that babies already dream in the womb. By observing the movements of the eye muscles, the researchers established that in the last months of pregnancy the unborn children alternate between phases of quiet sleep and REM sleep, the one characterized by rapid eye movements. "It is precisely in the REM phase that we dream. In the adult REM sleep is about 20% of total sleep, in the fetus it represents 60% and in the newborn about 50%.

In the REM phase, the infant's sleep is lighter and easily disturbed. Generally, after 45/60 minutes of deep sleep, the newborn begins to have agitation signals such as murmuring, movements and crying even while it is still sleeping. It is also possible for the baby to open its eyelids but if left undisturbed she could go back to sleep. Initially these steps can cause the baby to wake up and then take very short and frequent naps. The parents, in this phase of the infant's sleep, must avoid being the cause of awakening, maybe because they see the infant movements and noises they mistakenly think that the baby has finished its rest. Furthermore, it can also act to help the newborn to "link" the various stages of sleep together.

After the 3rd month, the phases of falling asleep and deeper sleep begin to be identified. At 6 months, each cycle lasts about 70 minutes and the cycles begin to concentrate mainly at night. At this age, non-REM sleep begins to differentiate into a light sleep phase and a deep sleep phase. Gradually, the cycles lengthen up to 90-120 minutes each in adults and are repeated 4-5 times per night for a total duration of about 8 hours.

Between the 1st and 6th month, a day-night rhythm progressively appears. The waking hours are initially distributed in the late afternoon and evening. The first sign of a circadian rhythmicity is precisely the appearance, at the end of the first month of life, of a long phase of wakefulness between 17 and 22. It is often identified as restless wakefulness and is associated with hunger or abdominal pain (colic). Starting from the 4th month, the baby begins to sleep for up to 6 continuous hours per night and is able to stay progressively more and more awake during the day. The total amount of sleep between 4 and 6 months on average drops to 12-14 hours, mainly distributed at night.

Between 6 months and 4 years, the sleep time is progressively reduced to 10-12 hours, divided between night sleep and daytime rest, with a progressive increase in wakefulness. At 1 year old, the child sleeps 13 hours overall, while between 3 and 4 years old he sleeps 12 hours. The daytime naps go from 3-4 in the infant to 2 towards 12 months, up to a single afternoon, longer, starting from 18 months. Around 8-9 months, there is often an increase in nocturnal awakenings, between 21 and 24 and between 3 and 6, which continues up to 2-3 years; 84% of children wake up at least once a night. These nocturnal awakenings are associated with a greater awareness of the world around them and the development of fantastic ideation, which involves the appearance of dreams and especially nightmares, which can cause sudden awakenings.

(We must remember the importance of proper sleep hygiene starting from the first months of life: children are habitual and good sleep is a condition that can be learned immediately. It is also of fundamental importance that a new parent knows the characteristics of the child's sleep to understand and adapt to his rhythms and to understand how and when these can be modified and how and when they must be respected).

Micro-Awakenings

We adults often wake up during the night between one sleep cycle and the next. Often, we don't even notice it, or we simply turn away to start a new cycle. The same thing happens to the newborn and to children in general, but more frequently (their cycles are shorter, therefore we speak of "micro-awakenings"). Often, they are not used to falling asleep on their own and therefore recall the adult to be supported: all this is absolutely normal, it depends on the fact that the little ones are frightened by the distance of the caregiver, a mechanism also present in the animal world and which constitutes a first defense of the puppies from the aggression of predators. During the first few weeks (about eight), babies wake up intermittently at night to feed before sleeping back. At this period, it is difficult and a bit advisable at all to sleep train the baby. This is due to the fact that at this stage, breastfeeding at night is important for the baby's feeding habit and also healthy growth. It is very important that the parent responds to the need of the baby for company, comfort and food. Several needs pertaining to baby sleep differs from individuals.

Moro Reflex

The Moro reflex is a neonatal reflex that manifests itself as a startle reaction, accompanied by the sudden opening of the arms and stretching of the legs. It is hypothesized that this reflex has the primary purpose of reacting in front of the perception of a danger or a sudden detachment of the mother and act precisely to keep her close. In practice, when the baby hears an unexpected sound or is left abruptly in a supine position on the changing table or in the crib, her makes movements as if trying to cling to something. Sometimes, after the Moro reflex, the baby will feel irritated or cry. The stimuli that can induce this reaction can also be murmurs on the face, or sensation of heat or cold in the abdomen.

Circadian rhythm

Every baby is different and some sleep through the night earlier than others, but it is vital to know that babies' biological clocks and sleep cycles are not the same as those of adults up to 1 year or older.

The first component of healthy sleep is respecting your child's circadian rhythms and to do this, you need to determine where the child biologically is.

Our biological clocks or internal clocks are genetically controlled. These clocks guide our circadian rhythms and tell our bodies when we should sleep (but also various physical, mental and behavioral changes).

They are largely inspired by our external environment with the main indication being dark (night) and light (day). These signals guide our internal clocks.

The circadian rhythm is a kind of biological clock, the period of 24 hours. Every day, in fact, certain conditions in our body, periodically, repeat themselves, such as the sleep-wake rhythm.

The term "circadian", coined by Franz Halberg, comes from the Latin "circa diem" and means "around the day".

The circadian clock is a complex internal system regulated by multiple factors and based on stimuli from the outside. For example, the rhythm of sleep awake is regulated based on the light and temperature of the environment.

This process controls the production of certain hormones and neurotransmitters that directly regulate brain activity.

Jeffrey C. Hall, Michael Rosbash and Michael W. Young, winners of the 2017 Nobel Prize for Medicine and Physiology, thanks to their studies, have been able to study our organism to understand the functionality of the circadian rhythm.

According to what they understood, each day is divided into 3-hour cycles, during which our body is led to do certain exercises or activities rather than others. Here is each phase of the circadian rhythm and its specificity.

The 3-hour cycles

— **6:00-8:59**

In this cycle the body gradually gets back into action. The production of the hormone that regulates sleep ceases, and cortisol levels increase, which leads the body to be in a state of alert. It is not recommended to do intense physical activity, because it would damage the body.

— **9:00-11:59**

The cortisol reaches its maximum and the body's state of concentration and activation is at its highest level. The most demanding tasks of the day would be optimal to do them in this period. This status will only be active until the lunch break.

— **12:00-14:59**

After eating, the digestive activity creates a generalized sense of sleepiness. Try not to drink alcohol on this cycle, and instead take a walk to digest, or a short siesta.

— **15:00-17:59**

You can concentrate on physical activity, since the body temperature rises naturally, and the heart and lungs reach their maximum efficiency. It is an optimal time if you want to enjoy the benefits of sport, without risking interfering with your night's rest.

– **18.00-20:59**

Time for dinner, but don't overdo it: the liver and intestines have a harder time digesting fats and sugars. The liver, however, will handle a drink better. It is also the ideal time to create and do new things.

– **21:00-23:59**

Melatonin begins to be produced, body temperature begins to drop, and it's time to get into bed. Avoid playing sports or staying on your smartphone if you want to have a healthy, restful sleep.

– **3:00-5:59 AM**

It is the last cycle, during which it is recommended to get to bed and enjoy a healthy restful sleep.

Circadian rhythm in babies

A newborn's sleep cycle is much simpler and has only two phases: quiet sleep and active sleep. Your baby's sleep cycle is much shorter, averaging 50-60 minutes for the first nine months or so, often even shorter.

When a baby falls asleep, it goes into active sleep, which is very similar to REM sleep for adults. During this stage, babies are also more likely to wake up. In this phase, a newborn will spend about 50% of his sleep cycles, unlike an adult, with only 20%.

About halfway through the sleep cycle, the baby falls into a peaceful sleep, characterized by slower, more rhythmic breathing, fewer movements, and no blinking. Quiet sleep is the end of the sleep cycle, which means that the baby will wake up or start a new sleep cycle on their own (or with a little help).

From six months onwards, babies develop multiple stages that resemble adults.

Routines

After some scientific (and perhaps a little boring data), I'll tell you about one of the most important things you can do to get your baby to sleep: routines.

They are fundamental because they allow the child to gradually get used to doing something.

Children like order, not only in the environment, but also in terms of the pace of actions. That is why it is so important to introduce daily and reassuring routines.

Paying attention to a newborn's hunger signal is a sign of respect as well as an instinct, but the same respect should also be given when faced with the requests for "order" and "regularity" of an older child.

In order for the bedtime ritual to be established in the child, it is important to be able to grasp the real signs of fatigue that it shows us, thus understanding if it is really time for bed.

A very important feature of a newborn's sleep is that the more tired it is, the worse it will sleep (sometimes it happens to us adults too). Never follow the rule "let's get her tired a little more so she sleeps better". In fact, by exceeding the threshold of tiredness, the body will develop adrenaline in order to continue to function despite the tiredness and this will make it difficult for the baby to fall asleep easily and sleep peacefully during the night. Babies in the first three months of life shouldn't stay awake for more than an hour and a half. If they can't sleep well during the day, it will also happen at night. For this reason, it is good to give the newborn the opportunity to fall asleep at the first signs of fatigue, that is when it:

- starts rubbing its eyes

- pulls its ears

- yawns

- stretches the body

- stares into space

- begin to focus less with its eyes, eyelids drop and it becomes less interested in the environment.

- whimpers and shows some irritability.

MORNING ROUTINE

Just as the bedtime routine, it is also important to have a daily routine.

Create an agenda and write down the child's habits: you can record its activities and the time in which these occur. For example: 7 AM wake up, 10 AM baby food, 12 AM rest and so on.

Obviously, the notes must be made according to the natural rhythms of the child. For example, you may note that at a certain time it becomes irritable and needs a feed or a diaper change.

Keep an alarm clock as fixed as you can so that your baby can get used to it as soon as possible (even if it will take some time) and don't let you wake up too many times at night.

If the child wakes up before the set time you can anticipate the time of the nap which, during the day, must be done in a slightly lit room so as to accustom it to the moments of day and night. Don't be afraid to make noise since the baby will have to get used to the surrounding world.

As soon as you wake up you will have to breastfeed and change it. Always dedicate 10-15 minutes to activities after feeding and changing nappies. Even if babies sleep a lot, they also need to be stimulated and the best way to do it is to hold them in your arms for a long time, cuddle them, talk to them and read or tell them stories; a baby sling or a baby carrier are also very useful as they allow you to carry the baby during the day, and therefore maintain an important contact with them for the so-called "bonding".

(The term bonding derives from the verb "to bond", which means "to bind, unite, weld, bind": it therefore refers to that special, deep and permanent emotional bond that exists between a mother and her child. Or, more generally, between parents and their child, because the father can also be happily involved. It is a deep bond, made up of intense looks, caresses and a thousand attentions, which allow you to take care of your little one, making it feel welcomed and protected. A bond that, once formed, lasts a lifetime).

Uplifting activities

Babies also need stimulation. The fact that they do not speak and that they sleep even 18-20 hours a day should not lead us to think that it is enough to treat them by doing the essential things: baby food, diaper, bedtime. These "practical" actions are important, but true care for a newborn occurs through contact, emotions, relationships, reciprocity and stimuli.

The first real stimulus that we can offer to a newborn, to stimulate both physical, cognitive and emotional development, is therefore to hold it in your arms, interact with it, make the baby feel contact: this type of parental education is called "high contact" or "parenting attachment" and the parents who practice it make a real difference in the future life of the child.

Children raised with high-contact parents are more confident, stronger, have better intellectual and physical performance, reach independence earlier.

Holding the baby in your arms, caressing them, cradling them and looking them in the eye: all these attachment activities develop in the baby not only self-confidence and the ability to perceive himself as "good", but also strengthen the respiratory activity, the immune defenses, the psychophysics of the child.

Objects

To learn about the world, children need to refine their eyesight and catalog objects, recognize sounds and noises, expand their sense of taste and smell, use touch to recognize and manipulate objects.

One of the simplest, yet most useful, games for a newborn is to provide them with colored satin ribbons, which they can take and pull.

It seems incredible but they attract children a lot: not only for their color, but for the possibility of being grasped and manipulated. In this way they stimulate hand-eye coordination and so-called fine motor skills.

As Montessori, an Italian physician and educator best known for the philosophy of education that bears her name, and her writing on scientific pedagogy, said that children have the potential to learn and the energy they use in their attempts to succeed is something extraordinary.

We know that infants sharpen their sense of sight progressively over the weeks. In the first days of life, newborns have a fairly limited vision and a preference for faces: they follow the face of their parents but focus at very short distances.

During the second month, large, vertical black lines can be drawn on a white sheet of paper. When the baby is in a state of quiet or active wakefulness, while she is in her crib (slightly raised) or you are holding her in your arms, it is the right time to show her the sheet with the lines, at a distance of 5.5 to 7.5 inches (the baby can focus at short distances). It will be completely mesmerized by them since she sees them as if they are moving.

From the third month on, you can give the baby a small pillow created with colored fabric and materials inside, such as laminated paper, which will tease the senses and the curiosity of the baby.

Maria Montessori, in order to develop the sense of sight, had developed in her method some moving merry-go-rounds (perfected by Munari, a famous artist and designer) to be placed on the babies' cradle.

Munari's carousel, composed of three sticks, a transparent sphere that reflects light and geometric shapes in black and white, helps the newborn, without the use of music, to concentrate, to focus on the shapes proposed and therefore to develop the sense of sight.

For newborns we can also offer "fabric" books or "quiet" books. They involve various senses and are therefore very important:

the sense of sight, thanks to their colors and simple and curious images or reflective mirrors; the sense of touch, because they often contain elements to be creased and manipulated, pulled, closed and stretched; the sense of hearing because they often emit small noises such as the rubbing of paper or extremely delicate music.

There are also children's specific mirrors on the market. They are very useful for the child, and the Montessori Method (mentioned above) has shown it: it does not have an aesthetic function, but a spatial one. It is used by the child to become aware of his body and its gestures, to practice the movements, to become aware of itself.

The baby will be able to see her reflection and many things will happen in the room: she will smile at the mirror and play in front of it!

Obviously, the mirror must be safe for the child and it should be placed away from them: it must not endanger them with the possibility that it could break or chip.

Other activities that we highly recommend for the baby are those called "Tummy Times" which help the baby to enhance its general motor skills. The babies will be prone positioned while awake and supervised, to encourage the neck and trunk muscles development and prevent skull deformations.

BEDTIME ROUTINE

There are several studies showing that children, of all genders and types and ages, benefit from having an organized routine throughout the day. And in fact, even in kindergartens and nurseries, precise routines are followed.

Your bedtime routine can include a bath (depending on your wishes whether to do it every day), a diaper change, a lullaby, a massage, breast feeding (every 2/3 hours since the body is constantly changing and will need a lot of energy).

This will help the baby to differentiate between the night and the day.

The bedtime routine should be started in about thirty to forty minutes before sleep and must follow a standard procedure that will be followed every night at exactly the same time. This will make the routine predictable and also relaxing. (Don't forget that, as soon as you notice signs of fatigue in your baby, to do not miss the chance and get your baby to bed right away).

The baby will wake up after 3/4 hours, even earlier sometimes and, during the day, it is better to wake it up if it sleeps too much.

It is well known that a nice warm bath before going to bed can help babies sleep. If your baby fears bath time, it is useful to wrap her in a warm towel and immerse her in water. This feeling of warmth and containment, in hot water, helps her to find the tranquility felt inside the mother's uterus.

After the bath, for the relaxation moment, you can choose an activity such as singing a sweet song to the baby, reading her a story, making her listen to the sound of an instrument.

Here are some ideas of sleep-baby sounds: a container where you can insert chickpeas or beans to swing so as to recreate a repetitive and relaxing sound; a bottle half filled with water; the triangle, whose sound is very relaxing.

Know that from the first two months of life, babies can recognize and distinguish the different melodies, making music a fundamental ally during moments of relaxation. 80% of children exposed to white noise (i.e. constant noise, without frequency jumps) fall asleep earlier than those not exposed, as we described in the previous section.

At this point our baby will be so tired and relaxed that it will fall asleep on its own. The more you do it, the more it will associate this routine with bedtime.

I would set up the routine with this generic pattern:

Abundant feeding before bedtime

In fact, the baby will sleep deeply with a full stomach and it is a good technique for those who don't want to wake up every 3 hours for breastfeeding.

In case of breastfeeding, you should not give the last bottle of the evening with artificial milk or additions like any type of biscuit because breast milk is already very nutritious and full of sugars. The biscuits are a concentrate of refined sugars and fats. The result will be having satiated the baby abundantly but also having provided them with a dose of extra energy, to make them more electric and irrepressible.

Avoid giving the baby chamomile tea before sleep: in fact, if given instead of milk or after the last feeding of the evening, it could have the opposite effect. It can act as a stimulant if drunk warm or cold (it calms only if it is hot) or it can make the baby vomit if swallowed after milk. Furthermore, the baby will quickly eliminate it by peeing and will still want to latch on to the mother's breast to drink or simply to seek a cuddle.

Giving the baby herbal teas, water or other liquids is not recommended, because there is the risk of interfering with the supply and demand mechanism that underlies milk production. In fact, the more the baby sucks, the more milk is produced. By offering the baby alternative liquids you will interfere with that perfect mechanism that guarantees the baby a nourishment that is always adequate to its needs.

Managing a small child can be very tiring, regardless of how they are fed and what you decide to do when they wake up at night. If you are not one of the few lucky ones with babies who wake up infrequently, it doesn't necessarily mean that getting up several times to rock them, sing lullabies or give bottles is necessarily easier than breastfeeding them. Not even if you delegate to the father: meanwhile, the little one does not necessarily accept the replacement (in the first months of life the mother "desire" is stronger than any other), and the hustle and bustle at home still risks keeping you awake.

The baby will probably wake up at night in the first three months and request to be fed. When it was in the belly, the baby was fed 24 hours a day, and it is natural that, immediately after birth, it feels the need to be fed the same way. The baby, after a few months, after waking up at night, will be more and more able to go back to sleep alone, without necessarily having to breastfeed.

Little burp

Why is it important to understand how to make a newborn burp and what it is?

When the baby sucks milk too quickly or, in the case of bottle feeding, when the baby's lips do not adhere perfectly to the nipple of the bottle, it is possible that, together with the milk, the baby also sucks some air, which ends up in the stomach, causing some discomfort the newborn.

The baby's burp, in fact, has the function of expelling the air trapped in the stomach which, if not expelled, can annoy the baby's tummy. Some children need to burp at every meal, even a couple of times by breaking the meal halfway, others don't do it very often. If the baby starts moaning during the meal, it can be a sign that her needs to burp.

Do not despair if, however helped, the baby does not burp, it is not always necessary. On the contrary, if necessary, the baby will let you understand, perhaps arching her back or showing restlessness immediately after feeding.

You can proceed as follows: put a cloth on your shoulder to avoid staining yourself in case of regurgitation, keep the baby straight and lightly tap her on the back. Be patient, because the burp can take up to ten minutes to wait.

If she doesn't, you can try this "foolproof" technique: put the baby on your lap, as straight as possible and, holding her head with one hand, raise her arms with the other to facilitate the opening of the ribcage, which helps the air expulsion.

If the baby falls asleep right after eating, don't worry and let her rest, she will burp when it wakes up or she might do it alone in her sleep. They can do from one to six, depending on how much air there is to expel.

The baby will burp for about four or six months, which is until milk is the main part of the baby's diet. As the digestive system matures and the baby is weaned, the need to burp decreases until it disappears completely.

The important thing, however, is always to observe the behavior of your child and decide accordingly.

Bedtime!

Obviously, there is no absolute right method or thing to do but you can try to set the bedtime between 6 PM and 7:30 PM. The baby will have a continuous sleep throughout the night if it goes to bed during this time slot. Small children need a lot of sleep and, since they have so much melatonin in their body, it would be inappropriate to give them this type of supplement.

Let's put the baby to bed where it will have to spend the night. Often children are put to sleep on the sofa or in the bed and then moved to their bed, and this can confuse them: waking up at night in a different place from where they fell asleep, they may feel scared and disoriented, and all this will make them more difficult to go back to sleep.

Try to put the baby to bed at the same time every day; this will greatly facilitate the possibility of the routine becoming fully established.

Do not force bedtime as it will be counterproductive and create stress for the baby.

(You can follow the advice described in the previous section on how to set up your baby's bedroom).

Activities before bedtime

Before going to bed it is best to put aside games that are sometimes too noisy and exciting. Leave only relaxing games and activities with which the children can play. Some games can be built at home at virtually no cost. Some, such as sensory bottles, are also suitable for younger children, others involve repetitive manual activities that promote concentration and relaxation.

Babies love habits. It does not matter at what time you put them to bed as long as this time is maintained regularly and the accompaniment to sleep is preceded by a series of actions that must be repeated over time.

The evening bath, which must be performed before the last feeding, is an excellent opportunity to strengthen the relationship with the parents and to help her relax. Hot water is very relaxing and the feeling of going to bed clean will be very pleasant for the child.

Plus, the moment before bed is perfect for whispering sweet words and talking calmly to the baby. There is nothing better than feeling the parents' company before going to bed.

You can also tell her a story or sing her a sweet lullaby.

Finally, you can rock her until she falls asleep, if she can't do it directly in the crib.

(Babies could choose a relaxing item that will help them sleep. For some it could be a broken blanket, a stuffed animal or a shirt. It is an important warm, soft and relaxing object that can "replace" the mother. For this reason, children look for this trusted object to fall asleep).

Communication between mom and dad

Despite this is not a real routine step, I think it is one of the most important points about baby management because communication is the universal solvent, capable of creating real miracles, when able to juggle with it.

Despite exemplary or mature a relationship may be, in a couple there will always be misunderstandings and arguments at home. However, we sometimes forget the presence of young children when this occurs, just as we forget the consequences this can have on their growth. Some advice may be, for example, not to limit yourself to speaking to your partner only for "service communications", such as "dinner is ready" or "we have to attend to that errand tomorrow".

Avoid centering all your conversations on the baby, worse if with nagging questions like "did you sterilize the bottle?" or "where did you put the pacifier?"

Strive to maintain an open and sincere dialogue, clearly communicate to your partner what is not working, what you don't like, what could be improved. Don't hide things and try to be as honest as possible with each other.

Do not underestimate the power of words which, especially in difficult situations, can be useful to express closeness, encouragement, understanding.

Advice to Help the Baby Sleep

Baby Sling

What calms the baby in its first months of life?

Everything that reminds it of intrauterine life. This sense of protection, of care, helps the baby for its development.

One thing that increases this sense of safety is the baby sling. In it, the baby is completely wrapped and is in close contact with the mother's body.

"Carrying" your child is one of the oldest methods of care, which in some places in the world fits perfectly with the needs of parents to move for work or other, thus combining the relational aspect with the purely practical. From one end of the continent to the other, in fact, babies have always been worn, albeit with different purposes, supports and methods, in relation to the culture of the country of origin.

The benefits of keeping the baby in contact with the parent's body are countless and have been known for some time.

Tests have shown that babies carried in their parents' arms cry 45% less than others, and that even in the worst evening hours, they hardly cry at all. Therefore, holding babies in your arms, or keeping them in contact with mothers' bodies, is good and absolutely welcome to consider as a sleeping aid for the baby.

Swaddling

Another strategy that can be used to make a baby fall asleep, based on the attempt to reproduce the conditions of intrauterine life, is the so-called swaddling, which consists in swaddling the baby to calm and reassure her in view of sleep. You can use special bands or simple squares of cotton muslin, as long as the fabric is not excessively warm (excess heat is one of the conditions to avoid to avoid the risk of death in the cot), that it is natural and breathable and that the child has the possibility to move her feet inside her "cocoon".

Swaddling is indicated in the first three months of the baby's life, when its need for containment is greatest and when the experience of gestation is still very recent for it. Subsequently, you can opt for a sleeping bag, which helps the child to feel "wrapped" anyway and keeps it warm even in winter, in total safety.

Cradling

By cradling we naturally mean swinging the baby in a slow and very delicate way, almost imperceptible.

How much cradling a baby can be a valid help to facilitate bedtime is a commonplace that has been handed down for generations, even if, so far, there has been no evidence of research on the matter.

Rocking the baby is the most common gesture that we all know and that helps the little one fall asleep soundly. It is important, in fact, that a newborn's sleep is deep and restorative and not everyone knows that cradling a baby helps to instill tranquility in her and, therefore, it improves the quality of her sleep. This is demonstrated by real scientific evidence confirmed by numerous researchers and pediatricians.

The practice of rocking the baby is also associated with its crying. In fact, cradling is also a way to console and relax the baby in the arms of the mother. In general, it is important for the mother to try firsthand to cradle the baby or to carefully follow the advice without too many second thoughts. It is important to try right away and not be discouraged if the baby does not fall asleep or calm down in the first few minutes of the swing.

Pacifier

The pacifier accompanies the first months of life of infants and the very first years of children, giving them calm and serenity and making their beddy-bye safer, with many benefits for the correct formation of mouth and palate. It's a valuable ally for parents who may not be able to live without it, as it's a great helper to put their babies to sleep.

The sucking reflex is innate and, already in the mother's womb, the baby sucks its thumb. Once it comes to light, the baby will instinctively look for its mother's nipple and start sucking.

Is this very instinct that allows the child to feed and it is always through sucking that it learns to coordinate breathing, swallowing and to stimulate the functionality of the face muscles. For the newborn, this natural reflection is of great importance and, at the same time, a real panacea. Sucking mom's nipple or a pacifier has a soothing and calming effect.

The general advice is to prefer pacifiers with orthodontic teat designed to favor the natural positioning of the tongue and to evenly distribute the pressure on the palate, actively favoring the correct development of the mouth. Both latex and silicone are harmless to the baby.

Latex is a natural and pleasantly soft material that, however, tends to wear out faster. Some newborns also have allergic reactions to the proteins in it. Silicone is harder and keeps the shape longer. With the first teeth, however, it is easily damaged.

The pacifiers can be of two materials: silicone and rubber (or latex).

There are three shapes available: anatomical, cherry and teardrop. The anatomical pacifier is shaped like a flattened drop and curved upwards; the cherry one has a round end; the teardrop one has an elongated and symmetrical shape.

In recent years, the most recommended is the anatomical pacifier whose shape seems to adapt better to the baby's palate, even if, at the moment, there are no studies that show real advantages of its use over the others.

The pacifier can be a very useful tool for calming most babies during a crying fit or for keeping good those who need to suck continuously; other children, instead, do not accept the pacifier and spit it out repeatedly. However, we must not abuse it and use it whenever the child cries: there is a risk of creating a sort of 'addiction'. The pacifier certainly helps to reassure the child and transmits security, but it is important that the parents try to understand its real needs, before indulging their baby's cry by giving it the beloved pacifier.

The pacifier does not "spoil" the baby, just use it with common sense and start removing it after one year of age.

Bed Clothes

One of the questions that mothers often ask themselves is that of having their baby dressed lightly or heavily during the night.

Trust your judgment and evaluate your baby's well-being when you put her to bed. For example, to check that the child is okay with the temperature, check the back of her neck, if it is sweaty it means she is too hot.

Instead of blankets you can use sleeping bags that have a well-defined ability to retain heat based on a special unit of measurement.

Singing to the newborn

Singing a lullaby to your crying child and struggling to fall asleep is a very ancient practice and is still present in very different cultures for geographic territory, language, traditions and history.

The calming power of the songs sung to your baby should not be underestimated. I'm not talking about playing a song from your cell phone but using your own voice. The little ones, in fact, prefer to listen to lullabies rather than adult songs, especially if sung by a female voice. It is not necessary to be good singers and in any case the mother's voice is certainly more pleasing to the children and to be preferred, because it brings true emotions. When babies are uncomfortable, try to sing instead of talking to them.

This will also strengthen your emotional connection with your baby, calm you down and make you feel a stronger union.

If, of course, you don't have the chance or the time (or the desire) to sing, you can always grab your phone and play songs on major websites. But remember not to bring the phone too close to the child, since it is an object that emits radiation. Furthermore, the less the child gets used to electronic tools, the better it will be for its health, like ours.

Try doing this even before actions your baby may not like, such as moving in the car seat, or being placed in the bathtub. In fact, starting to sing earlier will make the baby more relaxed and it will experience the moment in a less stressful way. (Remember, however, to always "explain" to the child, as I said previously, what you are going to do with it, if you have to move it from its position, etc).

Falling asleep in the car

The slight rocking motion of the machine can induce sleep in the infant and children in general. Scientists say that simple rocking, slow and delicate movements can cause those who are in a state of psycho-physical fatigue to fall asleep. Some even argue that the movement and hum of the machine can remind babies of when they were in mom's womb.

In a moving car there is always a gentle and constant hum from the car engine, which, as I explained a few sections ago, also represents a white noise, an uninteresting and constant type of noise that promotes sleep.

Various objects

Especially after the fifth month onwards, the child will pay more attention to the objects that surround it and, by imitation, will sometimes look for your objects. In particular, during the diaper change, the bath and other routine activities that could irritate the baby, we can give her some of our objects that will tend to calm her, such as a spoon, a comb, a toothbrush, etc. (objects that obviously will not be dangerous for it).

It can also happen that older babies get bored while eating in the highchair. Try to give them some items like the ones mentioned above so that they immediately get interested and no more irritable.

Chapter Three

Baby Sleep Training

Types of Training

S leep training is the process that parents use through various methods to help a child learn to fall asleep and stay asleep through the night. It is started around 4-6 months.

The three main approaches are:

- Let the baby cry (Ferber): typically, these methods suggest putting the baby to bed while she is still awake and allowing short periods of crying alternating with the parent comforting the baby but not picking her up. Ferber states that in order to fall asleep alone and sleep through the night, babies must learn to calm down.

- Tearless approach: a more gradual approach, calming the baby in sleep and immediately offering comfort when the baby cries (what we saw earlier in the text)

- Fade approach: parents gradually decrease their bedtime role by sitting next to the baby until she falls asleep and gradually moving the chair further away from the crib each night. Or even check on your baby and reassure her (without picking her up) every five minutes until she falls asleep.

As said before, the ideal time to start sleep train a baby is somewhere between four to six months. This is because training is associated with development. Training to sleep a 2-months old baby will amount to wasted effort because the body at this stage is still undergoing active brain development. At this stage, the baby lacks the ability to any training.

At four months of age, some babies go through sleep regression because the sleep cycle has changed. They experience longer periods of lighter sleep per cycle. This is the best time to work on independent sleep skills.

Other babies slumber derails around this time because they are working on new skills, like moving around and rolling. Some parents choose to wait until things are settle down before embarking on a sleep-training method, but you don't have to.

The age of your baby might determine what kind of sleep-training method you choose.

You could try a gentle shush-pat technique with a five-month-old, but you'll likely have to leave a one-year-old in the crib as they protest (cry or scream) about the new bedtime arrangement. So, remember to not attempt a formal sleep-training method before four months, until your baby is able to go longer in between feeds and their circadian rhythm starts to develop.

THE "SLEEP LADY SHUFFLE" METHOD

The method was created by an American woman, Kim West, the "sleep lady" and it is now "exported" to the world.

This method allows people to be guided by intuition, to recognize the behaviors of their children and to develop together changes that promote healthy sleep habits.

Each child is different and each parent has different educational techniques and methods, so the result of the program is unique for each family and each child; parents are accompanied in the process of implementing the program, which is based on scientific research.

In common with the famous (or infamous) Estivill Method (explained later), the Kim West Method shares the institution of a bedtime ritual, but the child is not left alone. Parents stay in the room at the beginning, sitting next to the crib or cot. The ideal age ranges from five months to five years.

Before five months, in fact, studies show that prolonged crying can create attachment problems. It usually takes about ten days to complete the process of less and less parenting until the baby develops the confidence and practice needed to fall asleep unaided.

The second element concerns the fact of creating an environment that promotes sleep, without too many toys or accessories.

The third point is precisely that of creating a routine, since children love repetition. They will in fact be much more serene and ready to go to sleep after the actions of the routine.

Once the routine has been established and the times have been set (for younger children, no more than four hours must pass between the last nap and sleep), it is time to put the baby to bed. The removal of the parent must be gradual. For the first three evenings, you sit next to your child, soothes her when needed with your voice and touch. On the following three evenings, however, you stay further away and use your voice if necessary. In the last three days, after putting the child to bed, you remain at the door until she falls asleep, aware that the crying will not last long, because the child has gone to bed when she is ready to sleep, reassured by the proximity of the mom or dad. One of the keywords of the West method, in fact, is "self-soothing" and it is one of the principles of education, because it teaches children how to deal with stress independently. This does not mean abandoning them to their fate but helping them to rely on their abilities. In the case of sleep, it is necessary to allow your child to orient himself by experimenting and thus finding the solution to fall asleep. Instead, going to her whenever she cries, it is a "reward" for those behaviors that should not be promoted.

It is essential to dedicate the right time to the method, as in all things.

The difficulty of sleeping could become a prophecy that comes true. Setting up and maintaining a method, on the other hand, is a strategy that also rewards when, perhaps due to an illness, teething, entering kindergarten or the onset of the first fears, it commonly happens that a child spends time in the parents' bed. The method "rules" are not followed in these extraordinary cases and parents will obviously have to comfort and support the child. But as soon as the extraordinary event ends, you have to resume your routine, doing your utmost to be able to completely restore it, even if it cost some negative emotion.

THE HOGG OR E.A.S.Y. METHOD

British nurse and pediatrician Tracy Hogg has devised a method to promote sleep in babies known as E.A.S.Y, from the initials of Eat, Activity, Sleep, You, described in the essay "The Secret Language of Babies". Hogg's approach is based on observing the natural rhythms of the child and the signals that the child sends to communicate their needs. By studying the baby's gestures, expressions and calls in the various phases of the day, the mother learns to interpret its needs and satisfy them quickly before the baby gets irritated, establishing a regular and reassuring cyclical trend. She feeds it, spends some time playing with it, cuddles it, puts it in his cradle at the first yawn (but without interrupting physical contact), stroking it and whispering in its ears and, finally, dedicates some time to her own rest and self-care, not to get too tired. Main feature of the E.A.S.Y. is the extreme elasticity.

Children love the regularity of schedules and the rituality of gestures, which have a reassuring effect. It is therefore useful to organize all aspects of care, from breastfeeding to bedtime, from play to bath, according to schedules that are as regular as possible, but not rigid, to meet every need and, at the same time, making the day's development predictable. In this way, in the evening, the little one will be more peaceful, relaxed and will fall asleep more easily.

CHECK AND CONSOLE METHOD
(also known as the Ferber method, gradual extinction, gradual waiting or interval method)

There are many variations on the check-and-console method, but the general principles are the same: you want to continue to check on your baby at set intervals but never feed or rock it to sleep because that would mean that you don't falls asleep alone.

After going through the bedtime routine, put your baby in the crib, leave the room and wait for a certain amount of time (let's say one minute). Then go inside and reassure your baby with sweet words like "mom takes care of you" or "I love you so much" or with some kind of touch, like a massage or a pat. Someone says that it is preferable not to pick up the baby. Others, however, argue that younger children need the presence of their parents to know that they have not been abandoned, especially if they have become frenzied and that this method can be applied from the seventh month onwards.

Continue to leave the baby and then check her, increasing the time between visits to about 10 or 15 minutes, and then continue until she falls asleep. When she wakes up, start the control intervals again.

This technique could take up to a week of work, but you should start to see some progress after few nights. Many experts recommend keeping a sleep formation log for reassurance. Some parents find that entering the room aggravates the child and may consider a more direct method, such as complete extinction or the Estivill method.

GRADUAL CRYING EXTINCTION METHOD OR ESTIVILL METHOD

The Estivill method was created on the basis of a system developed years earlier by the pediatrician Richard Ferber of Boston and published in the book "Solve Your Child's Sleep Problems".

The technique can be done in this way:

Introduce a routine to be repeated every night before falling asleep (for example, hot bath, pajamas, reading a story, etc.), then put the baby in the cot and leave the room, always strictly at the same time.

Return at progressively increasing intervals to comfort the baby (without lifting it). For example, on the first night, some scenarios require you to return first after three minutes, then after five minutes, and then every ten minutes until the baby falls asleep.

Every subsequent night, return at intervals longer than the night before. For example, the second night may call for returning first after five minutes, then after ten minutes, and thereafter each twelve minutes, until the baby is asleep.

The child will get used to being alone within a week.

Many associations globally warn of the possible risks associated with this unscientific method. Authoritative specialists have observed that a child who falls asleep exhausted by crying is not a well-trained child to sleep, but an exhausted child who ends up in apathy. Furthermore, children who are reassured by their mothers in times of crisis grow more peaceful and their sleep will certainly be better.

SCHEDULED AWAKENINGS

This technique is based on altering the baby sleep habits by waking it at prescribed times.

Here's the idea:

For one week, keep track of the times the baby wakes each night. Then, try to beat them to the punch. If the baby wakes at 12 and 4 AM, for instance, go in and wake them at 11:45 and 3:45 and rock them or do whatever you normally do.

Day by day, extend the waking times in 15-minute increments back to 12 and 4 AM, the to 12:15 and 4:15, and so on. The baby should stop waking on its own and instead wait for its parent, who has become their alarm clock.

As you add 15-minute increments between wakings, the baby learns to sleep for longer periods of time. Eventually you phase out the wakings altogether and find that your baby is sleeping through the night.

PROS: For infants who routinely awaken at predictable times during the night, the scheduled awakenings method can be a gentler alternative to Ferberizing; there is often less crying and parents feel a sense of control, since they are in charge of when the baby wakes up.

CONS: Parents have a hard time bringing themselves to actually wake the baby. Some sleep experts are adamantly opposed to this method and point out that there is little proof that its effective. They argue that an infants waking schedule is too varied for this technique to be effective. Another glitch is that this approach takes a while as long as it is done for three or four weeks.

REINFORCING SLEEP RHYTHMS

The gist of this preventive method is that you never let your baby (of 4 months or older) become overtired, because being too fatigued may be the root of the sleep problems. Instead, you anticipate your infants natural sleepiness and put her down at naptime and at bedtime accordingly. The approach works as follows:

Keep intervals of wakefulness brief when the baby is about 4 months old: every one to two hours put her down for a nap.

Older infants that can handle longer wakeful periods can be put down for naps two or three times a day. Any soothing bedtime ritual can be used, but avoid letting your baby nap on the run, such as in the car or stroller.

Anticipate when your baby will be sleepy. This may take a while.

Never wake a sleeping baby. Most babies (between 5 and 12 months) will take two or three naps of one to two hours a day, but longer naps will have no negative effect on night time sleep. The better a child sleeps during the day, the easier it is for them to fall asleep at night.

Set an early bedtime. Babies need to go to bed between 6 and 8 PM, depending on their nap schedule.

PROS: It's argued that with his approach, sleep problems won't develop and you will never need to resort to Ferberizing or other techniques; all you will need to do is predict when your baby will get tired and then let them sleep.

CONS: Never letting a baby become overtired and never waking them up can be harder than it sounds. While this approach may be less wrenching than some of the others, it's not a short-term quick fix: in order to work, you have to stick with it. If your infant is waking in the middle of the night, this method will only bring about slow, gradual change.

THE FAMILY BED

This method in which children share a bed with their parents is very common in many cultures and it is part of a child-rearing philosophy known in the U.S. as "attachment parenting." It's a sleeping style for getting a baby to sleep well, more than a technique. This approach should not be confused with the fact that sometimes your baby, in isolated cases, will "take refuge" in mom and dad's bed.

After the first months of life, when the child is able to tolerate physical detachment from the mother, it is right that she learns to sleep in her own bed, in her own room, and it is up to the parents to gently encourage her to detach. Sometimes it is mom and dad even more than the little one who seek shared sleep. And, by doing so, they risk creating habits that are difficult to change. The babies should learn to sleep on their own by the third year of age.

PROS: Proponents of cosleeping believe that the feeling of security the baby gets when she wakes up next to her mom and dad helps her go back to sleep right away. If the mom is breastfeeding, she barely has to open her eyes to feed her baby.

CONS: Many sleep experts offer warnings about this approach. You will have to forget about having any privacy. And there is the possibility that a parent will roll over on top of the baby. A family bed needs to be large enough to comfortably accommodate everybody and shouldn't have a soft mattress, fluffy pillows, or a comforter, which could suffocate the baby. Also, you should never consume alcohol or take any medications that could make you drowsy. In addition, when the baby is older, the problem of getting him used to sleep alone may be more difficult than expected.

THE CAMP METHOD

More than an articulated method like the others, it is a strategy to gradually accustom the child to the evening detachment from parents and to fall asleep alone in his bed without feeling abandoned. Initially, the mother or father 'camps' near the child's bed during the phase of falling asleep: you caress him or hold his hand, if the little one needs physical contact, or you talk to him or sing him a ditty. On the second night, the parent camps in the same room, but a little farther from the bed and then, gradually, farther and farther away, until they remain at the door of the bedroom. Finally, you put him to bed and leave the room.

This seems to be an excellent technique, to be applied gradually, taking into account the needs and times of each child. It is the system that most parents spontaneously use to help their child in a gentle and gradual detachment. Of course, it should be applied to children who are old enough to understand that their mother is not abandoning them, who goes into the next room, ready to intervene if they need her. The little ones of a few months are not able to understand this concept: for them, the mother vanishes into thin air when she leaves the field of vision.

Secrets from Baby Sleep Consultants

Here is a summary list of some of the most important things to do to get your baby to sleep

OVER TIRED BABIES BECOME HYPERACTIVE NOT SLEEPY!

Many children, when they are too tired, start screaming and crying inconsolably. When they reach this exasperated mood, it becomes even more complicated to get them to sleep. It would therefore be very important to be able to identify fatigue even before it manifests itself in a striking way. There are small clues that allow us to understand if children are tired, and which should lead us to dim the lights a little, speak softly, create an atmosphere of relaxation and pampering, to accompany them in their sleep.

POWER LIES IN THE ROUTINE

While these are probably old habits, they are by no means to be underestimated. Babies need routines and they are the result of the control you exert on the baby (obviously if you didn't put control over things, they would go at random). Children accept precise schedules and precise actions more willingly than you think, and this will definitely benefit the couple.

COUPLE WORK

The task of caring for the baby should not be completely relegated to the woman who will bear the burden completely. Teamwork will be essential for a couple's psychophysical balance.

The support of the partner becomes fundamental, which can be both practical and emotional. Sometimes, to relieve a critical situation, it may be sufficient to remove the partner from tasks such as cleaning the house or shopping. In other circumstances, however, the difficulties may concern the emotional and personal sphere: one does not feel up to the complex role of parent; the changes the body may have undergone during pregnancy have dealt a severe blow to one's self-esteem; the minor attentions of the partner make you feel alone and neglected. In all these cases, the other parent must never underestimate the partner's discomfort, but on the contrary must welcome and heal "the partner's wounds" by offering to listen to the outbursts and suggesting solutions to regain well-being. Sometimes reminding those who are close to us how much we love and esteem them can be enough to restore the necessary energy and make a smile reappear.

ENTERTAIN YOUR CHILD

Does the child receive the right stimuli during the day? If they sit for a long time without anyone entertaining them, they can get bored, a bit like we adults do. A little boredom is good, too much not so much.

Make sure to interact with the child when she is awake, read her a story, sing her songs, take her to the park, make her do suitable activities for her age.

Probably, in the evening you will have a tired, satisfied and ready to sleep baby.

DO NOT RUN IMMEDIATELY TO THE BABIES WHEN THEY CRY

Obviously, it is important to understand that nothing serious has happened to the crying baby and therefore you must not delay, but on the other hand you should not even run to the baby as soon as you hear a sound coming from her room.

DO NOT ELIMINATE ALL SOURCES OF LIGHT OR NOISE

Some parents try to make their children's room perfectly silent and dark. Just like excessive noise is not ideal, perfect silence and absolute darkness are not ideal either, because they will teach the child to wake up to every little sound they hear or every time there is a little light. The white noises in the baby's room help them not get used to excessive silence to sleep.

STOP BREASTFEEDING WILL NOT MAKE YOU NECESSARILY SLEEP BETTER

Breastfeeding is statistically related to a more fragmented night's sleep, with frequent interruptions by the infant to breastfeed. However, research also shows another interesting finding, which is that the total number of hours spent in a state of sleep by a nursing mother is higher than that of a mother who wakes up to offer formula.

This is both for a logistical fact (breast vs. formula preparation) but above all for a chemical effect, which allows the nursing mother to enjoy the production of oxytocin and tryptophan to go back to sleep immediately (which often does not happen to mothers who are not breastfeeding).

Conclusion

Raising a baby is certainly not a simple thing but it will certainly give you a lot of satisfaction (and some sleepless nights). The most important thing is to always remain in good communication with the baby, even when it grows up, establishing a good relationship with them, not based on overprotective possessiveness. Children are a being like us adults, they have feelings and understanding and they have the right to express themselves and exercise their self-determination, but they are a bit confused because of their new body and their whole new environment (how would you feel if a radical change occurred in your life?).

It takes some time to adapt and you will need to have a lot of patience. Always remember to explain to them what you are going to do and to talk to them in general. In the family, a calm and relaxed atmosphere should reign as much as possible, which is the main point for having a healthy baby who sleeps easily. Today's children will form the culture of tomorrow. They need as much help, love and support as possible to make it through.

You can compare babies to a blank sheet of paper, it will be up to you to decide what to write on them...

POTTY TRAINING

in 3 days

A Step-By-Step Guide to Help Your Toddlers Go Free from Diapers

by **Carol Moore**

Introduction

T ens of thousands of years ago there were no pre-birth courses or midwives who taught new parents the best way to put the diaper on their baby, indeed, the diaper didn't exist at all! Despite this, being able to "stem" the pee and poo of newborns has always been a problem that human beings have had to face since ancient times.

In warmer areas, children were left without clothes and mothers tried to promptly understand when their baby had to pee or poop while populations living in colder places had to cover their babies and ensure that they did not get dirty continually wearing heavy clothes.

In the most primitive civilizations, children wore animal skins which were then "stuffed" with moss and plants, materials which, once soiled, could easily be changed but which had poor absorbency and often caused skin problems.

In the Middle Ages, however, strips of linen were used as a diaper that were wrapped around the baby's pelvis and fixed with a safety pin.

In the following centuries, linen was replaced by cotton since it proved to be more robust and resistant to washing and with better heat dispersion, adapting more easily to the purpose. Cotton was the material of the "ciripà", a kind of absorbent triangle that takes its name from a population of Central America and their typical loincloths, which were wrapped around the baby and used as diapers.

Cotton was already an excellent material with a better absorbency than linen, but further progress was made in the mid 90's.

From the 1960s onwards, throughout Europe and North America, the first cellulose diapers were created together with a plastic pant that covered it. The latter, however, led to the creation of erythema in the child and therefore in the following years the quality of the diaper created only with cellulose was implemented. The diapers, however, were not disposable and were above all too bulky.

The greatest diffusion in North American and European markets occurred in 1961 thanks to Victor Mills, a chemical engineer, who for family needs, began working on this product in 1959 to launch it on the market years later.

Mills invented "Pampers" and he was the founder of the company that is still a leader in the sector. The spread of the "Diaper" product was rapid and is still considered a product that cannot be renounced.

Chapter One

1,2,3... go!

Is my baby ready to take the diaper off?

*T*he baby seems ready and we would like to free ourselves forever from the burden of the diaper and move on to the potty, but a thousand doubts are gripping us: will it be the right time? Will my baby be ready for the big step? Will it be difficult for him / her?

It is by no means certain that the elimination of the diaper must necessarily be a tragedy. We often worry excessively and instead the business turns out to be simpler than expected.

Removing the diaper is an important step, which is reached on average around 2 years of age. But, as almost always in these cases, this is a rough indication: there are more precocious children, who take off their diapers at 18 months, and others a little lazier, who can reach two and a half or three years. Usually, at this age the child begins to understand the meaning of poop and pee and is able to communicate when she is about to do it. It is the right time to start. If you go far beyond this term, perhaps you should get a hand from the pediatrician. Actually, to understand when it is time to remove the diaper, there are some signals that the baby unknowingly sends and that can therefore encourage us to embark on this adventure.

When the child is ready for the potty

The first thing to note is if the baby shows discomfort from the wet diaper. It is now big enough for you to understand without misunderstanding. If as a baby she cried desperately, now she will tell you plainly that having a wet thing on her ass is really boring.

An element to consider is the fact that you will find the diaper dry or almost dry in the morning. In fact, if your child has not urinated at all or just a little during the night, she may be ready to potty. The same thing is true after the 2 or 3 hours during the afternoon nap.

Another sign could be that the child begins to put objects back in their place and the appearance of the symbolic play on this theme; for example, children may start putting their toys on the potty or be drawn to stories about this topic. Their minds are preparing to consider the potty as an appropriate place for their "products".

When your child goes from climbing stairs with both feet on the same step to going up stairs alternating feet (around 3 and a half years old). She will have greater self-confidence and greater balance.

Most importantly, your child needs to demonstrate an interest and a willingness to learn how to use the potty.

If your child is interested in keeping safe or clean and is curious about what you're doing when you visit the bathroom and wants to wear "big kid" underwear, your child is probably ready to get going.

You will encourage this curiosity by reading children's books and watching videos about using the potty and talking about it while you go about your everyday parenting.

The child becomes aware of her own body: she then begins to indicate the wet diaper with her finger and names body parts and body functions.

The child has achieved autonomy in dressing and undressing and taking off the diaper.

All these preparatory signals must attract the parents' consideration, but they must not rush them into imposing the autonomy of the potty.

When the child is not ready for the potty

The parent may misunderstand some signs that could make them think that the right time for the potty has come and, therefore, anticipate the request for its use but stop shortly after due to the child's refusal.

In fact, the child can correctly pronounce the word "pee" and "poop" but this does not mean that she is ready to use the potty because first, it is necessary to connect these words to the actual experience of relieving herself.

A child is not ready when she absolutely does not want to have her diaper removed, if she persistently opposes the potty or the toilet, or if she appears annoyed when a parent watches her before pooing. Since she experiences this moment with discomfort, it could mean that she does not recognize her own feces or pee as good parts of herself or she might be annoyed by the smell or texture of her own physiological products.

First of all, it is good to understand the causes of this attitude, this rejection is often more frequent in children who have a more difficult personality or in overly permissive parents. It is a good idea to suspend potty training for some time and then try again after a few weeks.

If the child goes away to defecate and does not seem willing to share this experience, it could mean that she is not ready for the "big step" yet but it is necessary to wait a little longer. If you try to potty train before this time, you're likely to run into trouble.

Another sign that a parent could get is the fact that the child starts standing in front of the potty or takes off her diaper and does her business on the floor, or when she starts to sit on the floor with the diaper all dirty and seems happy with the feeling she gets.

If she is still struggling to walk and run, she is probably not ready for potty training.

Easy Transition

Even though we can never quite know when our child is ready, potty training is like any other milestone, which is why we recommend getting prepared well in advance to avoid unnecessary stress and worry. Summer is perhaps the favorite season for parents to help children achieve this first great achievement of autonomy.

In addition to some practical measures, to accompany the children in this delicate phase, it is necessary to ensure that the context in which the path is undertaken is adequate to facilitate the achievement of the goal.

CALM PERIOD

Precisely because it is a delicate step, it is better to propose the transition in a moment of serenity for the child, avoiding unfavorable concomitances with other change events, and therefore stress (because children love routines and are reassured by them). Therefore, it is not advisable to start the phase of eliminating the diaper during a trip, close to the birth of a sibling or the beginning of kindergarten.

You can also wait for the summer: everything is easier in this period because the child is easier to dress, she can wear only a pair of panties at home, so you will avoid doing many washes of dirty clothes full of pee. In addition, the child spends more time with us in the summer, so you will be able to maintain a constant guideline throughout the day.

If you notice a discomfort in the child, rather than a desire to grow and a peaceful acceptance of change, it is better to suspend the process and postpone it to better times, this may not be the right time, but maybe after a month everything is easier.

ASK THE CHILD

In addition to preparing the bathroom with all the accessories you will need (at this time it is recommended to involve the child), you can go and buy the potty with her. When the time comes, you can ask her if she prefers to use the potty or use the toilet. If she replies that she would prefer the toilet, I recommend that you also buy the reducer and a toilet ladder so that the child can climb independently. Furthermore, this latter accessory will allow her to rest her feet giving her security.

NO PRESSURE TO THE CHILD

The transition is important, but it is better to avoid that all the attention of parents, grandparents, uncles and siblings is concentrated on the baby's pee and poop. Too much attention can be an excessive load of pressures and expectations for the little one, making her feel uncomfortable with the risk that she will withdraw into her comfort zone, refusing to commit to removing the diaper.

Never scold your baby if there are any minor inconveniences but remind her that you just need to call mom or dad and go to the bathroom. The inconveniences during this period will be more or less frequent, it does not matter. The important thing is to face them with the right spirit.

FAMILIARIZE WITH THE WATER

From when the baby turns 6 months or generally from when she learns to sit, you can decide to start familiarizing her with the toilet, using for example a potty or a reducer. Parents will have the task of recognizing certain signs (certain expressions, gestures, or particular crying and sequences) that the child is preparing to poop or pee, even before she begins to speak. When these signs appear, parents can get used to taking the child to the bathroom, making using the potty or the toilet a normal and daily gesture, even if not always productive.

Observing siblings or older friends in this sense can also help. You can introduce the potty as if it were a game from 18/20 months. Make her familiar with it for example by placing it in the bathroom, inviting your child to sit on it while, at the same time, you sit on the toilet.

READINGS ON THE TOPIC

Poop and pee are very dear to children, widely addressed by gender literature with stories and illustrated books that prepare the little ones to manage their needs independently. Reading books on the subject to children is certainly fun and can be useful in preparing them to do without a diaper.

Thanks to their help, you can face with more serenity all the various changes that the growth process brings with it as well as the abandonment of the pacifier, the arrival of a little brother, the beginning of kindergarten. These are all important steps for our children, which can sometimes scare them and at the same time leave their parents without the right words to say. So, reading a good book on the subject together can reassure and help exorcise worries.

Don't forget to place these books near the potty and the toilet so the child can pick them up and browse them even while doing her business. A useful way to relax.

When she goes to the bathroom, even if we don't sit on the toilet ourselves, we can sit next to her without rushing her and trying to relax her. We can tell her a story or read her a book.

CORRECT USE OF PHRASES

When it is time to go to the bathroom use affirmations with modality choice rather than questions. Even if she is not the one to tell you, you will entice her more without the use of direct questions such as: "Do you have to go to the bathroom?", "Do you have to pee?" to which you might say no. So, it's better to use a statement like "it's time to go to the bathroom" and then continue with a choice proposal based on the statement just made like "do you prefer to go with mom or dad?".

DON'T LOSE IT

Parents must avoid engaging in potty-training battles; these could disrupt the parent-child relationship and delay sphincter control; furthermore, there is a risk of chronic constipation and encopresis.

Accidents along the way are to be taken into account and can be tiring for parents to manage. So, you will need to have lots of patience and some practical help. You should equip yourself with waterproof protectors for mattresses, rugs and sofas and plenty of spare clothing (I'll talk about it later in the text).

Be constant and supported throughout the day in this choice (nursery, nanny, grandparents, etc.); the child must be able to live this phase serenely and not have different lines of conduct based on the people he is with. The rule must be one and only one: "you pee in the bathroom and don't wear a diaper".

NO PRIZES NOR PUNISHMENTS

Reproaches, punishments and blackmail, as in all things in life, have only counterproductive effects. So, try to respect the time of the child (it is useless to rage, if she really does not feel the urge to pee maybe she is not ready). Rewards are also to be avoided: the greatest satisfaction for the child will be to be able to poop without the use of a diaper, like older children. So, it will be fine to give her great verbal acknowledgement when she succeeds in this new achievement.

(Many parenting manuals recommend using rewards and prizes to potty train your child. However, you might ask yourselves how useful rewards and punishments are in general in the education of a child.

According to common opinion, the "good" child is the one who does not mess around, that respects the rules, that does not scream, that does not throw tantrums. A child that pleases the parent is effect of their will and she is not using her own self-determination.

Some believes that children's education manuals are very centered on the needs of the adult, on the automatic acceptance and preference for the rights of the parent, almost completely neglecting to take the child's needs, feelings and evolution seriously.

As with education in general, even in potty training, the reward that is given to the child for pooping under your command can be a trap that turns herself against the parents.

So, you need to reflect on why the child sits on the potty or does her homework alone and if this responds to her physiological need, to her internal motivation, to please the parent or just to have a game or something sweet.

Probably, with the rewards system, you would have hit our goal, there and then, that is to make our little one pee in the right place, but subsequently you would risk that she expects a reward every time just for having responded to a physiological need.

Then, tired of candy, should we offer something else to her, promising her something different every time?

No, on the contrary. If the little one does not want to sit on the potty, there is a reason and must be investigated. Promising a reward would only mean shifting the child's motivation from a response to a physiological need to a desire to please the parent. Or worse, denying the existence of her need such as that of peeing, in favor of an action carried out only to get something else from the outside.

The biggest motivation that pushes the child to be independent of the diaper is not so much the rewards, but rather the desire and the fact of becoming like mom or dad, older brother or cousin a couple of years older.

It is the desire to do it alone, which is why the parent should help the child to do it by herself without replacing her.

Potty or Reducer?

The potty is a known object that traditionally is used to remove the diaper, while the reducer is instead a new object to many people, an accessory that, as the name suggests, allows to reduce the seating space of the toilet making it more comfortable for children.

Unlike the potty, the reducer is inserted directly on the edge of the toilet so the child can sit in peace imitating adults but feeling completely at ease.

Suitable for any shape of toilet bowl, the reducer fits easily and it is comfortable both for the child who feels great and serene when using the toilet, and for parents who are not forced to carry pee and poo from the potty to the toilet.

Switching from the diaper to the reducer on the adults' toilet can be very convenient, more hygienic and also strategic to convince those children who really want to become and imitate adults. Furthermore, going directly to the toilet allows children not to make intermediate steps and not to have problems while traveling if there is no potty available around.

The reducer, unlike the potty, is linked to the bathroom, so it has a certain and clear location. The reducers on the market now meet every type of need: they are soft, colored and more or less compact.

Obviously, it is necessary that the toilet with reducer can be reached with a stool and that also everything necessary for washing is child-friendly and within their reach. Same goes for clothes: more than ever during this phase, clothing must be comfortable and easy. The jumpsuit is fine while the buttons and zips waste too much time.

For some, though, the potty is necessary since babies who want to poop and pee outside the diaper also want to see what they leave behind them! For children, in fact, the toilet can be too big and too deep (the "black hole") and does not allow them to see their businesses and where they end up.

The potty can be introduced into the home almost like a game, also due to its shapes that often recall cartoons, animals or toy cars. It is certainly the ideal solution to remove the diaper permanently in a playful way without creating anxiety in the child: the child can use it independently, without access problems, being at its height unlike the reducer.

The potty has also a small ergonomic seat, made to measure for young children and a structure with rounded edges slightly raised in the back, to rest their back comfortably, and in the front, especially to avoid splashes if this accessory is used by novice boys.

It is definitely recommended for those babies who are starting to can't stand the diaper or for those who are afraid of the toilet depth. The potty moves easily around the house; even if it is advisable to keep it fixed in the bathroom. This will give clear indications to children on the place used for poop and pee. There are also travel potties models: there are inflatable ones or cardboard ones that can be assembled and disassembled in no time.

If you are undecided whether to use one or another, you could propose both alternatives to understand together what facilitates the child. This would allow her to choose without pressure and become aware of her stimuli in freedom and comfort.

IF THE CHILD REFUSES TO USE BOTH

There are some children who, however, refuse to use both the toilet and the toilet. In these extreme cases, potty training can be started from another place. Close one eye on hygiene and try to make the first pee in the bidet, or in a basin or in a vase. If you have open space, you can propose to do it outside. Do not worry, this imaginative and atypical approach will last very little, and soon the children will be the first to want to go back to the bathroom voluntarily.

Little trick

One of the tricks that you can use to make your child go to the bathroom when she plays and do not want to stop is to ask her directly "do you want to go to the potty or the toilet?"

instead of the usual "Do you have to pee?". You can continue to ask the question this way, even though the child always continues to choose the potty. In this way she feels that she is the one who decides, and as every parent of a 2/3 years-old child knows, the sense of independence and the desire to decide on their own is one of the most evident characteristics of this age.

POTTY

Pros

It is child friendly

The child often feels at ease because she can decide to sit alone

Helps the sense of independence

You can move it anywhere in the house

Cons

It must be emptied and cleaned after each use

It is not always available away from home, with friends, in a pizzeria, in a restaurant, etc.

At some point you have to agree to abandon it to start using the toilet

REDUCER

Pros

It is easily transportable by car and ready for use even outside home

You can leverage the child's instinct to imitate and show her how to do it

It is something that even adults use, and therefore the child can accept to use it more easily

You don't have to empty and clean it

Cons

Some children feel inhibited using it

Some children are afraid of falling into the toilet

Young children (1 year and a little over) need help climbing on the stool and sitting down on the toilet

Essential Things

One of the secrets of potty training is to make sure that you have all the necessary items and supplies before you begin. Start with these and build up your child's interest in potty training.

This list of supplies will support you and your child to make this developmental milestone easier.

In the Bathroom
Potty Chair

Stand-alone potties are the right size for small learners and are available in a range of colors and familiar cartoon characters. A kid-sized potty is more straightforward to use and less daunting than a conventional toilet and can be moved around the house if necessary.

Seat Reducer

Smaller and cheaper than a potty chair, the seat reducer (or potty seat) sits on top of a conventional toilet and reduces it to a child-friendly level. Many of them have cheerful patterns and a padded pillow for added comfort. There are also folding versions that can be used both in public toilets and in emergency situations, but also for the home toilet. But beware that it is not always very stable and sometimes you have to keep the reducer still.

Stool

A small plastic or wooden stool can help your child get up and sit down on the toilet. It will also give your child a feeling of safety and security, so it will help you get her in the right place to use the toilet. A stool is also useful for lifting kids to the sink to wash their faces.

Toilet Paper / Flushable Wipes

Toilet paper is already standard in your loo but try to pick up a pack or two of flushable wipes. These are similar to baby wipes but disintegrate more quickly and are safer for plumbing. These wet wipes are softer than toilet papers, they are more familiar to your kids and make cleaning easier. Only make sure they are compatible with your plumbing.

Kid-Friendly Hand Soap

Potty training includes teaching good hygiene, so select a hand soap that facilitates post-potty hand washing. Try stocking up on foaming soap instead of a regular bar or liquid soap. Toddlers love bubbles, and there are simple, cheap recipes online to make your own once you've got a pump dispenser.

For Your Child

Choosing a potty is necessary, but so also is outfitting your little potty trainer for the job. From motivational undies to easy-to-remove pants, here are the things you need for your potty-training baby.

Awesome Undies

Cool potty-training pants and big-kid underwear can be a great motivator to help your child progress past diapers; anticipation is a crucial component of positive potty training. Imagine taking your potty trainer to the store with you to pick out her first pack of various colors, patterns, characters, and themes.

Easy On-And-Off Pants

During the first few days, weeks, and months of potty training, ditch the rompers, overalls, and button-up jeans for simple on-off pants and elastic waist shorts. Avoid using drawstrings or zippers to stop pants because they would need to be untied and unzipped. Your child will always have the impression that she needs to go, so you don't want to waste any time giving her complicated clothes; you want your child to be able to get the pants off in the shortest time possible, either by yourself or by your child. The goal is to teach your child to be self-sufficient enough to take off her pants and use the toilet, so pick a style that is easy enough for her to handle.

Training Underpants

Potty training pants in disposable and reusable/washable models are intended to make your child feel comfortable (unlike a diaper). That way, she knows when the potty is out, but the wetness is contained so that it doesn't soak into the clothing. For some families, training pants are a required intermediate phase in the potty-training process; for others, they may be a crutch that prolongs the transition from diapers to underwear.

Progress Chart

The use of a potty is a whole new habit for your kid, and it will help if she can see, chart, and remember her progress. There are a lot of beautiful charts that you can purchase on the web or print for free, but a simple hand-drawn grid decorated with your child should work. The goal is to help her — and you — note all the achievements that have been accomplished.

For Bedtime

Nighttime Potty-Training Underpants

Standard training pants are still not absorbent enough to accommodate an overnight period of 8 to 10 hours. Nighttime training underwear is more porous than their regular counterparts and is available in both disposable and reusable/washable models. They're a valuable transition item when your child works on daytime potty training as they can replace diapers.

Protective Mattress Cover

Sheets can be cleaned, and you can take care of an accident, but a soiled mattress is not an easy job to clean. Prevent this issue by purchasing a waterproof mattress cover: some are in plastic, and others have a light cotton top and a waterproof bottom sheet. Mattress covers may fit tightly over corners like a fitted sheet or wrap like a saddle around the middle of the mattress. Try investing in at least two covers to cope quickly with nighttime injuries.

Extra Sheets

Buy two or three sheets. Take a hint from seasoned parents and make a bed with at least two layers of sheets and a waterproof mattress cover. This way, if an incident happens in the middle of the night, you can easily take off the dirty sheet and the top layer of the protector and tuck your little one back into the bed with the dry bottom layer. Accidents happen, so you're going to save yourself from middle-of-the-night "fun."

Other Interesting Products That Will Help You
Pee Clock

There is a watch on the market that reminds the baby through lights and sounds when it is time to go pee. The music can be set in time intervals of 30, 60 or 90 minutes. It is very useful to prevent the first "accidents" that can happen to the baby who is trying to remove the diaper.

Mini Toilet

There are small toilets made especially for small children, complete with toilet paper and easy to clean, some also equipped with accompanying music.

Unique Potty-Only Activities

Whether your child has difficulty understanding the simple idea of going to the potty, is scared of the potty or is unable to spend enough time in the toilet, there is a wide range of potty training books, videos, and toys to make the potty cycle feel more familiar and less scary. Set down one or two books or toys that your kid would enjoy or find motivational books (which feature favorite characters in potty training) and dolls (which go potty or sing dumb songs about going number two). If you want to turn over your smartphone or tablet to your toilet trainer (which is not recommended as a daily practice), make sure to have a childproof cover and a screen protector that is waterproof like the new iPotty, a stand-alone potty with built-in iPad holder. However, be sure to follow the American Academy of Pediatrics' media guidelines, which do not prescribe a screen time for children under two and restrict the screen time to two hours a day for older children.

Stickers in the Toilet

It can help for boys to place funny stickers inside the toilet and encourage children to hit the stickers. Many parents want to start the boys in a sitting position, but if you want to encourage your son to urinate while standing, a specific toilet target may be a helpful device. These go inside the potty to ensure your little boy's target is the toilet bowl and not the walls. You may also select a cheaper option. A simple scrap of toilet paper may provide an amusing goal, when placed at the bottom of the potty. This is for boys who may need some motivation to aim.

Potty Training Rewards

New behaviors can be strengthened by encouraging accomplishments (although I personally disagree).

Start small with stickers, kid-safe sweets or all-natural fruit snacks, or some other little treat to make potty improvement. Brand-new potty trainers will need an incentive for every small victory (we're talking several times a day), but once your child has learned the basics, set long-term targets (five days without incidents, 25-time peering, etc.) to reward them with a prize.

Playing Area

Try to create a play area for children in the bathroom. Insert a small bookcase, a drawer with games, etc. so that even in the bathroom there will be a space dedicated to the child who will entertain herself while having fun. This will inevitably increase her affinity towards the area and can make her interested in the use of the toilet. This will help you enormously and with minimal effort.

Chapter Two

Potty Training

Potty Train your Child in 3 Days

You've finally decided that your child is ready to get out of diapers, CONGRATULATIONS!

The use of the toilet is a valuable skill that further strengthens your child's independence and increases her confidence. Toilet training aims to teach your children how to understand the pressure they feel in their bodies and when they need to use the toilet.

The most significant thing to remember is that potty training is a process, and your child will have many accidents, but stick to this approach, and your child will use the potty regularly in just three days.

Is Your Child Ready?

Before you decide to take a plunge and a potty train, you will familiarize your child with the use of the toilet. Let your child come to the bathroom with you and show her what "big boys" and girls are doing.

Most of the kids are excited to learn about the bathroom etiquette. Show them how to wash the toilet and how to wash their hands. Look for signs of preparation and anticipation, such as your child telling you when he or she needs to pee or poop, asking you to use a potty, feeling irritated with a dirty diaper.

Does your child seem ready to use a potty? The three-day strategy will work only if your child is on board.

Choose the Weekend

You'll need three days in a row when you're at home with your kids. For working parents, this approach works better on a weekend of three days or at a time when you can take a day off work to add to a daily Saturday / Sunday.

You'll be inside for most of the weekend, so it's important to brace yourself mentally to give a lot of time with your kids. Have fun with them. If you can't schedule out three days, on the last day, speak to your childcare provider about what you've been doing and ask them to continue the cycle.

Stock Up

When your child shows signs of preparation, take them to the store and pick up the underwear together. Buying underwear with their favorite characters is a fun way to get them excited about wearing big boys or big girl underwear.

Also, if you're going to spend a lot of time at home, you may want to think about some home improvements in advance. This could be art supplies, movies, sports, cooking, baking, or something else that keeps you and your child entertained.

Before the Long Weekend

Let your child know one week in advance that it's time to say "goodbye" to the diapers. Depending on what your family chooses, this could be a complete farewell or a partial farewell where diapers or pull-ups are used at nap and bedtime. When you start practicing, underwear must be worn at all times when your child is asleep.

If you're going to make a complete goodbye to the diapers, you should count the remaining diapers with your child and let them know that when they're gone, there's no more. It would help if you also made sure that only one diaper is left before bedtime the night before you start your toilet training.

Share the cycle with your spouse and other parents, such as nannies, babysitters, and family. Take turns (especially if there is an older brother) or stay together and support each other throughout the process.

It is vital that all adults are involved in the process and that the use of the toilet does not become something that can only be done with one person in the family. By sharing responsibility, your child learns that they need to use the bathroom with everyone, not just in certain circumstances or with particular adults.

Day 1, Day 2 and Day 3

DAY 1

Right when your child wakes, remove him or her from the diaper. On the first day, let the baby go around the house naked. This situation, which children generally love, will allow them to come into contact with their body and its needs.

You can opt to place a little potty in the living room for quick access. This is your choice, as some people might want to leave all the bathroom practices in the toilet. Give your child a huge cup of water, milk, or juice so that they have to pee regularly. Have a constant sippy cup within reach of your kids. Give your child a lot of liquid and look for signs that your child is about to pee or poop.

When you see the sign, take your child to the bathroom to use the toilet immediately. About every twenty minutes ask them if they prefer to do it in the potty or in the toilet (with the reducer). You might want to set an audible 20-minute timer so that your child knows that when the timer goes off, it's time to try using the toilet. Tell your child how to unfasten their pants, clean up after a toilet, and wash their hands. Clearly you will be the one to carry out these tasks, however listening to your words will slowly bring her closer to this ritual. In books or among some videos available online you will find songs and nursery rhymes to accompany this precious moment.

Before lunch, it's a good idea to go to the bathroom together. "I always have to pee before lunch and dinner. Let's do it together, then wash our hands and go eat." Encourage the child to sit on the potty while you are sitting on the toilet. after being in the bathroom, wash your hands and go eat.

After lunch, keep an eye on her to see if she struggles to evacuate. It is common for children to poop after lunch if they haven't done it in the morning.

Before napping or going to sleep, tell your child it is time to use the potty (avoid asking whether or not she wants to use it). Put on a diaper before falling asleep to avoid accidents. You can also choose to put her to bed without a diaper, it depends on what results you got in the morning. If you have put on a diaper, take it off when the baby wakes up.

If you wake the baby and the diaper or the bed are dry, praise her (if you have chosen to use the rewards technique reward her with a pebble or sticker). By the time there are three dry naps, the baby will have made great progress. After bed, take her to the bathroom and sit on the toilet while she is sitting on the potty. So, start introducing the habit: after bedtime you go to the bathroom.

Before dinner, follow the same procedure as for lunch.

Then follow the usual evening ritual, for example toothbrushing, pajamas, a little TV and reading a fairy tale. It is a moment of relaxation when you may want to pee. Keep the potty close at hand.

And when it's bedtime, tell the baby that all people sit on the potty or the toilet before going to bed to say goodnight to the last pee of the day. This also serves to establish a habit.

If your child does not desire to try, you could say that we're going to try "after you've finished playing with your toys," or, if your kids know numbers, you might say, "we're going to try when the clock says 10:00".

Try to use the bathroom at every changing phase of daily actions, for example after cleaning a toy/material, before a snack or lunch, and before and after a nap and bedtime. This will eventually become part of their daily routine.

Remember to use emotionally neutral behavioral observations about your child's progress. "You peed in the toilet, that's where the pee should be" or, "You peed on the floor? Let us clean it up together."

When the child is able to evacuate 10-12 times in the potty it means that she is becoming independent.

Hurray, she did it!

Celebrate the baby but don't overdo it or embarrass her.

You know your child best. Some children react well to an exciting celebration of achievement, while others are not at ease in this regard. If they react well to rewards, maybe your child would be excited about stickers or small treats (you can do a reward chart to encourage her potty training).

DAY 2

After the first day, you can use the diaper at night in order to avoid accidents.

The cycle for Day 2 and Day 3 is the same as Day 1. Some people stay inside for three days to solidify the process. On the second day, in fact, you can add another step: going outside for a walk with the child. Wait until your child has peed in the potty and then go out immediately. When leaving the house, make sure your child is wearing baggy pants with nothing underneath. They must not wear diapers or underwear. Your goal is to get out and back home without peeing on and without having to use the potty when you are out.

Think that in the East children are dressed in cotton shorts with a cut in the middle so that the little one can do his business anywhere in an agile way and be washed immediately, without the impediment of clothes. When you go outside, go to a park or do an activity nearby, and please remember to take a small portable potty with you in case your child fails to use the public toilet, as some children do. Expect accidents to happen. Only change the underwear as they happen, and don't make a big deal. Say to them, "We pee and poop in the potty."

DAY 3

The potty should be part of everyday life at this point. The day should go something like this:

— wake up, take off the diaper and potty within five minutes

— hand washing and breakfast

— clothes and teeth washing

— activities around the house or walk (after an hour and a half or two remind the child if she needs a potty)

— invitation to the potty before lunch and hand washing

— invitation to the potty before the afternoon nap. Put the diaper on before going to sleep. Sleep for about an hour

— wake up the baby and remove the diaper. Have her sit on the potty and leave her for three to four minutes (if she prefers you can stay with her in the bathroom to keep her company)

— afternoon ride. Potty before going out and after returning home

— dinner. Tell the child how proud of her you are

— after dinner, play quietly

- potty and baby bath

- fairy tales or TV, then potty before bed

- brush your teeth, last visit to the potty before bedtime. Put the diaper back on the night just before you say goodnight

If you don't get good results right away, wait about 6 to 8 weeks to try again. This is a technique that requires a lot of patience and time, but it will work

Potty Training Tips

Let your child use the toilet before leaving home and immediately after arriving at their destination.

Bring multiple changes of clothes and underwear before you leave.

Inform teachers, daycare providers, nannies, and babysitters of the signals from your child when he or she wants to use the potty and the words you use at home so that they can be familiar with your desires (i.e., pee, poop, toilet, potty, doo doo, BM as Bowel Movement, tinkle, etc.).

Going without a diaper is a new experience and some children can feel awkward or scary. Stay calm and encourage your child in this cycle. Research has shown that a negative response or punishment after an accident may contribute to a negative connection with pee or poo and may impede improvement.

Believe in the process. It's very tempting to get upset on Day 2 when your child has an accident, but if you do it on Day 3 and beyond, your child can show you that she knows what it means to be potty trained.

You can also use an "if, then" statement to your advantage. "If you're going potty, then you can play in the park." Choose a spot you know your child loves, like a playground or a ball pit. Think about all the fun things they like to do in there beforehand. Be very disciplined while there and tell them they have to potty before they play. (This is a good strategy if they have to go potty and they have to interrupt the play).

When they hesitate, tell them you're going home so they can't pee or poo on the playground equipment. Allow them to change their minds, but if they still refuse to go — and this is the most essential part — then go home.

Teaching to wash hands effectively

Washing your hands, even if before it was an important practice, now more than ever it has become a mandatory rule.

Children have the habit of touching many objects and then putting their hands in their mouths, but unfortunately the hands are an important vehicle for the transmission of germs and bacteria responsible for colds, flu, gastrointestinal diseases and more.

It is advisable to wash your hands before meals, after playing, after pooping or peeing, after sneezing or after returning home.

First of all, check that all the accessories that will be used for cleaning are present, such as non-aggressive hand soap suitable for children's skin, towel and a ladder to facilitate the baby in washing.

— - Start by washing the baby's hands with water that is not too cold or hot

— - Put the soap on the baby's hands (preferably liquid because the classic soap could retain germs) and begin to lather the back of the hand, fingers and nails for at least 30 seconds (there are those who even reach 60 seconds), singing a song to make the moment pass a little more playful and cheerful

— - rinse hands thoroughly with running water to remove any trace of soap that may be left under the nails

— - remember not to touch the tap with your hands (especially if you are in a public bathroom) and dry your baby's hands with a clean towel or an air dryer

In short, washing hands can be considered a kind of do-it-yourself vaccine, simple, cheap and without side effects.

Eating Habits and Diet

Give your child high fiber foods, such as fruit and vegetables, wheat bread, and high fiber cereals, to obtain the right stool consistency. It is common for children to be "picky" eaters during the toddler era.

It is important to never miss fruit and vegetables from your table and to have a diet as varied as possible. If children are exposed from early childhood to a wide variety of foods and flavors, the more likely they are to enjoy them.

Here are some ideas that could benefit you:

If your child doesn't like food, give small portions and praise to your child for trying one or two bites.

Restrict milk to 16 ounces of low-fat milk and, if constipated, restrict all dairy products.

Provide fresh fruit instead of sweets and snacks.

Actually, children are able to regulate themselves by taking the amount of food they need, so you shouldn't force them or scold them if they don't want to eat. The energy requirement varies from child to child, based on the pace of growth, weight and activity she does, so it is good not to get anxious about this subject.

Even at this stage, your child's diet must be as varied as possible, it is better to limit the amount of sugar and salt and favor simple cooking, without too much fat. The best dressing is extra virgin olive oil used raw. Be careful not to use food as a reward or consolation and teach your children to sit at the table and avoid letting them eat in front of the TV or while playing.

Better to prefer steam cooking, excellent for vegetables and fish, because it reduces nutritional losses, or in the oven, which allows you to cook without adding fat. Even pressure cooking, speeding up preparation times, reduces the dispersion of nutrients. And if the vegetables are boiled, keep in mind that salts and vitamins pass into the cooking water, which can be reused to prepare soups or cook pasta.

It would also be useful to eliminate (or at least limit) the following foods from the diet of children:

- – - French fries, which contain a carcinogen that forms during cooking

- – - gummy candies, which are full of sugars, dyes and jelly, toxic substances

- – - fruit juices, a product that contains many added sugars (it would be better to choose a 100% fruit product)

- – - carbonated and sugary drinks, for the reasons mentioned above.

Montessori Approach

I would like to refer to one of the fundamental figure of Italian and world pedagogist of the twentieth century because I think she did an amazing job on children, Maria Montessori. Mother of Scientific Pedagogy, she was also the creator of the "Children's Houses" and had exported her method all over the world.

She was also an active supporter of the battles for women's emancipation, for the recognition of the rights of people with deficits, the poor and the exploited.

A multifaceted woman that dedicated herself to study and research for the improvement of society through education, with the hope of being able to build, through it, a world of peace.

To help the baby to eliminate the diaper, first of all, ask yourself if she wants to remove it and how you can help her in this achievement. This is because in the Montessori philosophy the importance of the child and her self-determination is always placed at the center.

Referring back to the basic principles of Maria Montessori's thought, we can say that it will be fundamental:

Follow the child, her speed and her needs;

Love the child, show affection, offer strong emotional support;

Stimulate and encourage her to search for independence;

Create a suitable prepared environment.

If the child does not progress, going back is absolutely not a defeat. The child is likely to be focusing on improving some other skill.

The child will understand for herself when the right time has come and will let us understand. We must favor the child and not judge her. This will increase self-esteem and self-confidence and then face the surrounding world.

Here are some Montessori tips for getting rid of the diaper

— take advantage of the *right* moment when the child is ready and not according to the season. It is important not to postpone that moment

— always change the diaper in the bathroom since the child will identify this place with her physical needs

— change the diaper in an upright position, this is because the child will associate the position with taking off her panties, as well as the fact that it is much more comfortable for her (make sure the baby can support herself on her legs).

— go to the bathroom with her or take her to the bathroom if she wishes

Going to the bathroom and using the toilet must become a natural thing and must not be a mysterious circumstance. She will observe through the example of his parents. Feeling close to someone will somewhat eliminate the stress when you have to do something for the first few times.

It is advisable to avoid sitting on the toilet as an obligation even though many parents leave their children sitting as a punishment until they do their business. On the contrary, Montessori recommends waiting for a warning gesture that indicates that they want to go to the bathroom.

− create a space for the baby in the bathroom

as I said before, it is important to create a suitable bathroom area for the child in which she can feel comfortable. You can add the potty, children's books that she can browse freely.

Montessori explains that to take advantage of their autonomy, it is important that children do not feel that they have to depend on others to solve their problem. If you have a potty, a stepladder to use the toilet, or a reducer, it's important that they find them within easy reach. When they understand that they want to and that they can go there alone, it will be easier for them to do so, if everything is ready

− avoid rewards technique

The child is reaching part of her natural development and this is not a special action, a talent or a mission that deserves to be rewarded

— do not scold her or make negative comments

This is absolutely to be avoided. I will never repeat this concept enough: with children it pays to be patient, to be loving and not to be angry at their apparent clumsiness. The motivation towards success must prevail in this path. Try not to give importance to the event, teaching it without taking it back and without causing further agitation in them. Children need to understand that this is a normal growth process and, when they feel wet, they will naturally predispose to use the potty.

If we set out to take the path of removing the diaper, it is useless for us to take it as a commitment with an exact deadline. We allow children to go at their own speed.

Chapter Three

How to Fix Problems

Potty Training Regression

*T*he development of children, in every sphere of life, never follows a straight line, never always and only goes forward, but it may happen that for a certain period it stops or that some steps can be taken backwards.

This also happens with regard to the acquisition of sphincter skills: suddenly, after months and months from having eliminated the diaper, when the control of one's own needs had become the normality for the child, accidents return frequent and parents are understandably alarmed.

To distinguish whether it is a simple accident or a small phase of regression, it is first of all good to understand if the child had already manifested in some way that she had to go to the bathroom and, for a matter of timing, she was unable to hold it or if the "accident" (or more than one) occurred without any previous signal.

In the first case it can happen even if you are not going through a regressive phase, simply due to the fact that children have times and rhythms that do not always coincide with those of adults; in the second case, especially in the presence of repeated accidents, one could speak of regression.

But don't worry about that. Regression can be corrected. It's just going to require some retraining, patience, and listening to get back on track.

What Can Parents Do to Help?

Even though your child seems to have mastered going to the potty, a new situation can throw them away. Their attention and energy are on the new thing, not on staying dry and finding a bathroom. They may also lose interest temporarily once they have mastered the potty, especially if there was a lot of fanfare and attention to toilet training. In reality, so-called regression is a fairly common phenomenon. In fact, the development of the child is not linear and always ordered.

Regression can sometimes happen to older children, too. Changing schools or bully can trigger a setback. Children who are mentally and emotionally overwhelmed may ignore the signal of their body to head to the bathroom.

Accidents can happen when a child is under stress. Anything new or different can also cause extreme stress for children. These situations may lead to a regression: a new sibling, new school, a different kindergarten, a new parent routine, social changes in the family, etc.

This stress can be minor and temporary, just like when your child is exhausted or distracted by playing.

Here are some of my advice to help your children:

STAY CALM

Even though you're frustrated, remember that a period of regression can be normal. It could happen for several reasons, but it can be fixed.

DON'T PUNISH

Experts say that punishing your child for bed-wetting or any accident is only a backfire. Bedwetting, in particular, is not under your child's control. And punishing accidents makes it more likely that your child will try to avoid punishment by hiding or trying not to poop or pee at all, leading to constipation and even more accidents.

CONTROL

Check the baby's pee as much as possible by making her go to the bathroom at set times such as when she wakes up, after breakfast, before going out, before going to sleep.

OFFER POSITIVE REINFORCEMENT

Clean up accidents and move on. Give your child the attention they want to take to other good habits: at preschool, at the table, washing their hands, etc.

It feels great for any of us to hear that we're doing the right thing. Give a lot of hugs, kisses, and cuddling. A sticker chart or a treat after a successful toilet stop works well for some children as well.

FIND OUT WHY

Accidents in older children are often linked to a lack of control over the child's environment. Try to get into their heads and find out what's going on. Understanding the cause can help you figure out the solution. Talk it through and open up the issue.

SYMPATHIZE

You should recognize that you know it's hard to keep up with everything that's going on in your child's life. You can use a childhood story about a time when you regressed and tell them that it can be normal.

REINFORCE TRAINING

Remember, what you did before initially worked. You can reinforce that with a set time to sit on the potty. It may be before nap time or after the bath or mealtime. Make it part of your routine. Endeavor not to make a big deal about using the toilet and don't force the issue, add it to your child's day.

MAKE EXPECTATIONS CLEAR

Make your child know that you expect them to return to the potty and to have clean undies. Let them know that you know they can do this.

DON'T MAKE COMPARISONS

Avoid making comparisons with other babies by saying for example: "Look, Tommy has already taken off his diaper! What are you waiting for?".

Don't compare your daughter to her brother, her little cousin, her classmates. And don't allow it to others either. Each child is a unique, unrepeatable person. This will lead to negative effects on both the self-esteem and the serenity of the child, who instead needs to compare only to herself to be more aware of her own potential and progress.

If the child is confronted with a positive thing, she may feel the need to always be the best for fear of disappointing. Conversely, if compared to a negative thing, she will get frustrated and will end up hating the person she was associated with.

This tendency to always be under judgment feeds the fear, anxiety and shame of children, emotions that accompany their lives and that break down their self-confidence.

SEE YOUR DOCTOR

Give your pediatrician details of the regression. You want to prevent the possibility of infection and make sure you're on the right track.

Language

Cute and technical language are both fine.

During potty training sessions, parents often wonder what kind of terms they should use with children. Is language such as "bowel movements" or "urine" proper, or should parents use more informal terms such as poop and pee?

Whether to use clinically correct terms for body parts or digestive waste, is a highly personal decision and often based on one's family history, people whose parents used "pee" and "poop" are likely to use these terms with their children.

Nothing is wrong with either style. You're not going to do any injustice or harming your child by using childish words to describe these things. She is a child, after all, and unless you're planning to hide her away, she will finally learn both the correct words and some slang that will make you absolutely cringe.

I think it is not the use of words but most of all the embarrassment that a parent makes the child feel about his or her private parts or about having to evacuate that can cause the child to become inhibited.

Potty Language Should Not Be a Language of Shame

As I said before, as a parent, you shouldn't associate nudity or the baby's private parts with something embarrassing or ashaming. This could cause unjustified embarrassment in the child who will be reluctant to show her genitals to pee or poop, thus delaying her adaptation to using the potty.

My dispassionate advice is to use any term you want without showing bad emotions such as anger, anxiety, resentment etc.

How to Manage Bedwetting

All children get the bed wet sooner or later during the night. But how can this problem be solved?

It can take some time for your baby to learn to stay dry all night. The process that leads to knowing how to control the bladder usually takes place around the age of 3/4, but up to the age of 5, bedwetting should not be considered a concern.

However, when it happens it is stressful for the child and frustrating for the parents. However, the family can intervene with some precautions to try to avoid (or at least contain) the phenomenon. The important thing is to always remember that you should not make the child feel guilty, but you must try to reassure her and make her feel more confident, so that she will undertake not to wet the bed.

A contributing factor to bedwetting is the fact that the child has a deeper sleep than adults. This means that, while the adult that has a full bladder, still feels the urge to urinate and wakes up to go to the bathroom, the child sleeps in such a deep sleep that she does not feel this stimulus and therefore gets wet. In addition, the baby's tissues retain more fluids than adults and are able to absorb a fair amount of water which then flows into the bladder.

Instead, psychological factors alone can facilitate its occurrence but are not the cause of bedwetting. Problems at school, arguments between parents, a move, the birth of a baby brother are stressful events that can give rise to various psychosomatic disorders: some children may express their discomfort with recurrent abdominal pain, others with vomiting and still others with enuresis.

Here are some of the tips I can give you if this problem happens.

– First of all, it is important to establish a dialogue with the child and possibly you can talk to her about your experience when you were little. Communication with the child is always fundamental and it is right not to forget the episode. By doing so, the child feels and is sure that the problem is resolved at some point. You have stopped having it in bed after all. Also, your child will feel less embarrassed by talking about it.

Always be comprehensive and be a reassuring figure to her as much as possible.

You can also explain to her the technical reasons that led to bed wetting. Obviously, providing more understanding on this subject will help.

- Another reason could be the fact that she drinks a lot before bedtime and therefore, a solution, to limit drinks the two hours before sleep (especially liquids that promote diuresis). Although it cannot be considered a definitive solution and although it is not always practicable, limiting the consumption of drinks, especially carbonated, in the hours preceding the moment of sleep, can help to contain the problem. It is important, however, that the child drinks enough and regularly throughout the day.

- You can train her bladder to make it larger. In fact, among the possible causes of enuresis, there is that of having a low capacity of containment of the bladder which tends to empty as soon as it reaches the maximum filling.

In these cases, the child can get used to 'hold' the pee for a longer period of time during the day, extending the interval between two successive excretions, so that even at night the holding period can increase.

- The use of absorbent panties is particularly useful since, on the one hand it allows the child to have a peaceful sleep and, on the other hand reduces the stress of parents who are not forced to wash sheets and pajamas every morning.

Remember always to empower the child without having to resort to useless scolding and above all without making her feel ashamed, getting help in cleaning and changing sheets. This helps the child to feel she can contribute positively.

- Even if you have the urge to wake her up in the middle of the night to make her pee, this is not recommended. However, some parents, before going to sleep around 23-24, wake up the child (from 5 or 6 years old) and take them to the bathroom to pee.

Despite the child must be able to enjoy adequate quantity and quality of sleep, remind her to always go to the bathroom before going to bed.

- You can also create a calendar with dry nights and wet nights and stick stickers on it and remember to praise her if she left the bed dry.

Alarm systems are also used, especially in the Nordic countries, to warn the baby when she is getting wet. It consists of two parts, an extremely sensitive control unit that uses the most advanced electronic techniques, and a lightweight and comfortable detector pad that is placed on the mattress cover and the sheets, then covered with a smaller sheet. As soon as the first drops of urine touch the pad, the alarm emits a loud sound that wakes the child. It is a system that works quite well, but which in many countries is reserved for children who do not respond to other treatments because it associates enuresis with a nuisance stimulus, sometimes interpreted as a bit punitive. In fact, it is usually the last resort.

Do not think about reusing diapers anymore.

How to eliminate stains and odors

First of all, know that there is a way to prevent your baby from dirtying frequently. In fact, there are absorbent sleepers on the market that you will have to place practically everywhere (in the bed, on the sofa, in the car) and always carry some with you until your child is independent. There are also washable ones, cheaper and certainly less polluting in the long run.

This will allow you not to lose our temper if an "accident" occurs and you will be able to continue this transition period in the most rational way possible.

In addition to removing urine stains and related halos on clothes, mattresses and perhaps the car upholstery, remember that you will also need to eliminate the persistent stench.

Here is the procedure to remove stains with the help of household products:

1. Dilute some hand laundry detergent in cold water and blot stains. You can pour the resulting solution into a spray bottle for convenience.

2. Mix water and white vinegar in equal proportions. Blot or steam the area to be treated.

3. If you have forgotten or did not have time to treat the stain before and it is already dry, sprinkle it with baking soda and leave it on for the whole night; allow at least 12 hours to pass, then remove the grains with a brush and proceed with the normal washing.

4. If you are facing a stain that does not want to go away, you can combine the mixture of water and white vinegar with baking soda; first proceed with the powder and then with the liquid solution, let the mixture act and remove it only when it is completely dry.

Borax may be possibly used for this purpose. It is produced by the reaction between boric acid and soda. Before using it, clean the area with a mild stain remover. Immediately after, sprinkle some borax on the patch and stick some paper towels well. After about half a day, remove the borax residue and move on to washing.

MATTRESS

The most important thing to do in case the mattress is wet with pee is to absorb the stain as much as possible. If the stain is fresh on a material that cannot be submerged in water, the very first thing to do is to dab the stain with dry cotton rags and press it to remove as much liquid as possible. The area must be buffered and not rubbed, in order to prevent the urine from penetrating even deeper or worse still from spreading. Only then can you proceed to treat the stain with the methods described above.

When the rags no longer get wet from the stain contact, we can begin to disinfect the area with a solution made up half of hydrogen peroxide and half of white vinegar. In this way we obtain a very powerful disinfectant which also has the advantage of deodorizing. The solution should be dabbed on the stain with other clean cotton rags until you no longer smell the stench.

If, on the other hand, the fabric can be removed and washed, you can only do the first step indicated and then you can throw everything in the washing machine.

While if the pee is already dry or the stain is already dry, proceed directly with the bicarbonate mix and a mixture of water and vinegar. At the end of this operation, make sure that the mattress is dry. If necessary, use a hair dryer or fan.

If the yellow stain is present, when the disinfection is finished, it must be removed with only hydrogen peroxide that is rubbed with a white patch and then it can be left to dry directly on the fabric, perhaps with the help of a low temperature hairdryer to speed up the operation increase the whitening effect of hydrogen peroxide.

CARPETS

Not much can be done on carpets, but you can still give it a try in the laundry.

If the stain has been done recently, however, you can proceed in this way:

Sprinkle the stained area with baking soda or corn starch until it is completely covered. Leave it there for as long as possible (24 hours would be perfect) and then scrub with a soft bristled brush. You will understand if the process has been successful because grains will form which must then be removed.

However, if the damage seems particularly serious, mix the baking soda (or corn starch) with cold water and rub it on the stain trying to avoid damaging the texture of the carpet.

The method just described is also valid for car interiors or any other type of upholstery, as well as for the pee of any pets.

CLOTHES

Again, if the stain is recent, the first thing to do is to dab to remove most of the urine.

When it comes to clothes, it will be necessary to use something that disinfects and at the same time has the ability to deodorize. Create a mixture of 12vol peroxide and white vinegar in equal parts and tap the stain until it disappears. But be careful not to overdo it: the result could be a nice yellow spot.

If this happens accidentally, add a whitening product to your usual detergent in the washing machine. Try not to use the dryer because the heat would end up fixing the stain even more.

For light-colored fabrics such as white ones, it is better to opt for a pre-wash with hydrogen peroxide: not only is it stain-remover but it is also a disinfectant. Just use it in combination with water (in a proportion of 1/6, so for a tablespoon of hydrogen peroxide we will use 6 of water). In the absence of hydrogen peroxide, it is also fine to use vinegar, in slightly higher proportions.

Training panties - a great help

They are simply a wonderful invention for parents who are having problems with potty training. With them you can say goodbye to diaper rash, eczema, irritation and all the problems from transition to the toilet in a natural way.

One type of panty resembles the diaper. This model is made of a special sponge that absorbs just enough so as not to get the legs and feet of babies wet and prevent them from feeling discomfort (the absorbency depends on the amount of urine) and a waterproof outer layer. They are perfect when you are away from home and you are not sure to get to the toilet on time, such as during car trips but also during naps. They can be removed and put back on. These panties leave the baby feeling wet to let her know that it would be better to go to the bathroom just after the stimulus.

There are also ecological models with the internal absorbent layer and the one in contact with the skin made of breathable cotton and corn starch, while the elastic containment bands and adhesive parts are made of recyclable plastic. Definitely a good way to reduce pollution.

The other model is less bulky than the first, has less absorption capacity and has a non-waterproof outer layer. This special panty can be suitable for those children who want to tell parents when to go to the bathroom but who involuntarily lose a few drops of pee (not suitable for heavy losses). They are very comfortable to take off and put back on and allow the child ample freedom of movement.

The baby doesn't want to leave the diaper

Taking off the diaper is an achievement that has different times and ways.

For most children this happens quite naturally, almost abruptly. Parents ask her to say when she needs to pee, they invite her to use the potty or the toilet directly with the reducer and it may take a couple of days to do so, if the child is ready.

For other children the path is more difficult. There is a sort of affection to the diaper, which gives security.

It can be a ploy to take off her diaper and put her panties on. The child, pissing herself off, will perceive a sense of annoyance so next time she may think about it before doing it or warn her parents.

But each child is unique. Precisely for this reason, it may happen that your little one will hold his pee for 24 hours, consciously, in order not to use the potty.

It can also happen to put her on the potty, to spend a lot of time humming, playing and chatting without getting anywhere.

When she can no longer hold her pee, she will invoke the diaper. If she is put on the toilet, she won't do it anyway. Small gimmicks such as tickling or running water will not stimulate urination.

If you are stubborn and don't allow the baby to use the diaper, she will eventually pee herself off, crying desperately.

Very often, the refusal of the potty is due to trauma. Specifically, something scared the baby, giving her insecurity the first few times when she took off the diaper.

It takes very little to traumatize the child. She may, in fact, have heard a door slam while on the potty, a reprimand if she wet her panties, etc.

Precisely for this reason, the best thing to do is to have a lot of patience. When the child is on the potty, you have to create a relaxed environment and have to be careful of noises, moderating the tone of voice.

Then, avoid insisting and try to converse with her. Don't worry too much if a lot of time goes by without the baby peeing.

Surely, in this delicate phase the child should not be reproached when she gets dirty, otherwise she will close herself off even more and everything will become difficult. Rather, let's praise her when she can understand the urge and go to the bathroom, encourage her with every little step forward.

That said, it is obviously normal to be 'forced' to give a diaper at some point, otherwise the kidneys and bladder would be put to the test.

Problems with poop

Every mother knows their babies well and will be able to recognize when they are forcing themselves in wanting to eliminate the diaper early. You must always take into account the progress of the child, but at the same time, do not insist too much and do not have too many expectations, trying to see how things are progressing as you go along.

It can happen that the child is in difficulty and rejects the urge to poo, or because they get dirty without a diaper or because, for example, they are forced to stop playing to reach the potty. In these cases, a constipation problem can occur. It takes a lot of calm and tolerance, even here it is essential not to put pressure on the child, otherwise you risk doing worse. You can wait up to 2/3 days of abstinence, then it will be necessary to stimulate the child with a glycerin suppository: at that point the advice is to put her on the potty, keep her company by playing or reading a story until she has done the poo.

Some babies may develop a form of stool retention and ask to use the diaper again. However, if they use it as if it were a potty, for example by hiding while they poop and using it only when they poop, it is good to give it to them. They are still doing the correct "gesture" and will soon be ready to sit on the potty.

For the child, feces represent a part of himself that often struggles to let go.

A technique that can be used if you see the child in difficulty with their poop is to create a moment of play, for example by proposing suitable readings for their age, leaving the children in their intimacy and showing you available only if they request it.

Another strategy is to participate with them in the joy of what they have produced, to let go of the feces and greet them. This is a small action that gives peace of mind to the child who peacefully detaches herself from her "product" and which is taken into consideration by the parent.

These are some hygiene rules that might help:

— get your child used to going to the bathroom at the same time every day;

- make her sit on the potty, or on the toilet with the help of a reducer and a stool, so that her feet are well supported and assume the correct position a little squatting;

- if, with the first attempts to remove the diaper, you understand that the child is reluctant to evacuate, it is better to take a step back and put the diaper back on for a few more weeks;

- do not keep the baby sitting on the toilet or potty for too long: if after about ten minutes she does not evacuate, better try again after a few hours.

In addition, you can tell the child who is trying to poop, making some effort: "dear, you are feeling this way because it is your poop that is asking you to let it out. Let it out. Only you can help it with that."

So, let's give the child power over their own bodies. Obviously, this is a different approach to manipulation or distraction to doing something only to please parents or make them happy.

Also try to dampen the child's performance anxiety, avoiding calling grandmothers, aunts and various relatives to ask if the child has pooped. Thus, monopolizing attention will make things more difficult and hinder them.

I advise you to buy low-cost underwear so as to be more relaxed if you have to throw some of them away.

To improve the child's defecation, avoid external intrusive maneuvers such as microenemas or external stimulations, unless they are advised by the pediatrician and always follow his help. This will cause the child to lose body awareness and mastery will worsen. The more you make your baby poop artificially, the harder it is for her to become familiar with that mechanism.

Sometimes a child may feel sorry for their poop going down the pipe. In fact, at the beginning it is good to use the potty so that the child looks at her products and can reassure herself. You can explain the process that happens to poop after it has ended up in the sewers. For example, you can tell her that through a long journey it reaches the sea to feed the fish, or that it is transported and used to fertilize the surrounding fields and trees. Probably with these explanations she will better deal with the "loss".

Hard Stools

We talk about constipation when the feces are hard and appear as pebbles (goat feces). The child may feel a lot of discomfort or pain during evacuation and the stools may show traces of blood due to the rupture of blood vessels in the anal region during their passage.

To identify constipation in children you also observe that there is no bowel movement for 2 or 3 days longer than usual, bowel movements are hard or painful, stools are large and can clog the toilet, or, as we said before, there are drops of blood on the external stool.

The fear of seeing these episodes repeat themselves in the bathroom pushes children to try to avoid defecating at all costs. The more they hold it, the more the feces dehydrate until they become real stones.

The presence of occasional constipation should not cause concern, but it is important to consult the pediatrician when the situation tends to become chronic and if bowel movements with the presence of blood tend to be frequent.

A temporary intestinal obstruction can result from a minor trauma that caused the baby to poop in a somewhat painful way. That's why she is scared and may hold back from doing it.

One thing your pediatrician might recommend is to give your child special syrups to make their stools softer and more voluminous.

Other things that can help the transit of feces are to increase the intake of fiber, therefore fruit and vegetables. Since this can also happen due to not drinking enough, get your child used to drinking more throughout the day. Avoid packaged foods or foods that have undergone a long process of transformation. You can add a glass of warm water with lemon to your child's diet and let her drink it every morning.

Prevent your child from having a too sedentary life and make her do physical activity. Just take it to the park and let her run for hours. The movement, in fact, facilitates intestinal evacuation.

Problems with pee

Keeping the pee and poo, which the child reaches around 2/3 years, represents a very important evolutionary stage like weaning. The child learns control over herself and begins to listen to what she needs without the parent telling her. Being a very delicate phase, it should be faced by the parent with patience and serenity. The fact that the child holds on to pee or poop could be seen as holding back emotions and the reason should be investigated.

Criticizing her, judging her and making her feel "dirty" is wrong and absolutely to be avoided. The baby will get frustrated, so you better do not pile it on. Do not associate the idea of urination with something bad, to be abhorred. The result will be that "if it is a dirty thing it will be better to hold it". It would be advisable to change your mind and make the child understand that peeing and pooping are not negative events, but they are nice things to do because they free themselves and feel better. You can ask the baby just as she evacuates if she feels better or worse. Surely the parent's behavior is not deceptive but pointing out your child as a "slob" is to be avoided.

Always remember to praise the baby who goes to the bathroom, singing her funny songs that she will associate with a happy and carefree moment.

Remember not to reward or punish preschool children, especially on things that affect the child's body such as food and toileting. This is normal and physiological. If instead it becomes something that the child does to please the parents, remember that then she can use the same method with you: she may not go to the bathroom so the parents "do not win" or to keep attention on her. This, from a physiological fact, passes to the relational field. Instead, you can empower the child by telling her that pee and poop are her stuff and they, if she wants, can be managed together with the parent.

Right after pooping or peeing, instead of telling her she was good, say "Wow! You saw how better it feels! Even mom feels a lot better when she does it".

Always rely on your pediatrician especially if you think the problem comes from a more serious cause (such as a urinary tract infection) and try to detect when the disorder has emerged. So, you will understand if there was a trigger or not.

Fear of the toilet or washing hands

Fear of getting dirty is common in children and can represent an excessive attempt to control one's body. This excessive control can arise from difficult emotional management. An emotional condition that is difficult to control may be present in the child, which is expressed in self-control behaviors from which the excessive fear of getting dirty arises.

It is usually an anxiety that disappears naturally with the passing of development.

More frequent, however, for preschool children (and also in many adults!) is to be afraid of the toilet and therefore refuses to pee and poop there. What can parents do to face this seemingly inexplicable fear?

First of all, it is important to understand that it is not so obvious for a child to immediately achieve good sphincter control: this developmental phase is complex and requires many resources. Children may fear falling into the toilet or being sucked into it in some way, so they struggle to evacuate safely.

To tackle this problem, we must certainly not ignore this signal.

As I have repeated several times in this book, it is always advisable to convey naturalness when in the bathroom, involving the child in various tasks and making her familiar with it, creating a kind of play and fun. For example, you could have her use the toilet brush as a "weapon" or have her flush the toilet.

You can also take dolls or puppets to the bathroom so that she feels reassured. You could also personify the toilet by greeting it; this would create greater confidence with the object.

You must always avoid, when the child poops, to use words like "that stinks" and "that disgusting", children do not want to feel stinky and above all they do not want to do something that disgusts their mother. So, when the baby evacuates, you have to praise her and tell her that she was a good girl and her mother is very proud of her.

Problems and Solutions

Understanding if you need to take your baby's diaper off is never very easy. There are parents who are based on age, but in reality, the best thing to do would be to rely on certain cues your child gives you every day.

Not noticing whether the baby is ready or not

You need to have good ability to observe the signals and not get anxious about having to eliminate the diaper, perhaps on the advice of the pediatrician or some friend.

Some may recommend that you continue the process once it has begun while others may recommend that you have the diaper put on again if your baby is still not quite ready.

If the child suddenly finds herself having to perform a task for which she does not feel ready yet, anxieties and fears could easily emerge. These would lead the child to even refuse to do her needs for hours (frequent is the case of children who become constipated precisely because they experienced the transition to the potty as a stretch).

In addition to this, a study in the early 1950s highlighted how, in the transition phase to the use of the toilet, not only the maturity reached, but also the temperament of the child, which the authors divide into 3 categories: easy, slow to warm up and lively / difficult.

While the easy child adapts quickly and without much difficulty to the changes, the slow-warming child will need slower rhythms and more reserved situations to reach her goal. The lively / difficult child will have a lot of difficulty adapting to the demands of the environment, will be irritable and more unpredictable, especially in the rhythm and signaling of her needs.

I advise you, always as far as possible, according to your availability of time and desire, to wait for everyone to be ready for the process. As a result, everything will be simpler and more harmonious.

Do not communicate with the baby

One can make the mistake, often due to too much haste, of not preparing the child calmly and in time, for example by providing her with books to consult or by telling her stories.

In the transition period from diaper to toilet, you can start by presenting the potty as a game and not an imposition or a challenge to be overcome in the shortest possible time. Keep in mind that the baby does not know why she has to do it, since the diaper has been one of her most faithful companions since she was born: she has the right to know why she has to change.

Once you have entered the topic, you will move on to practice. It will be a pleasant and fun time to choose the potty or the reducer with the favorite shapes or colors of the child and maybe it would be better to do some tests with water first or with a doll with which you can simulate the use of the reducer.

In addition, sitting on the toilet and showing how to use it will be an excellent incentive to use the reducer.

Sudden events that cause regression

Events such as a parent's business trip, or the birth of a sibling, or a change of home can all be reasons that could lead the child to wet the bed again at night.

However, this shouldn't make you more alarmed than expected as even up to 5 years of age it is normal to pee in bed.

Always treat it very calmly and don't make the child feel wrong.

Better not to wait for the entrance to kindergarten

When it comes to determining what is the best time to start the transition to the toilet, many families passively let external events determine it such as entry to kindergarten, where teachers are not required to change diapers, or in the vicinity of particular events, such as trips or moves or the return to work of one or both parents.

Yet, the moment in which you will have to switch to underwear is a passage that will at some point mark each individual life. It is advisable to set up your daily actions and habits so that you become familiar with the potty or the toilet right away.

As we said before, children can get used to sitting on the toilet or on the reducer since they are able to stand by themselves in this position. It does not matter where: the child is more independently on the potty, while the toilet with the reducer is a rather complex destination to climb and always requires the help of an adult.

Or, when possible, you can also try to set up a toilet routine. Therefore, you can associate the use of the toilet at particular times of the day: as soon as you wake up, before going out or going to bed, in the middle of the morning and after an afternoon nap.

Parental Behavior

For parents and especially for mothers, this phase can be very stressful and can jeopardize the harmony of the home environment.

Sometimes it is possible to become filled with doubts that can cause frustration. It is normal to think that the correct actions are not being done or that you have not waited long enough etc. Things get more difficult if the baby is unmanageable due to the fact that she is complaining or crying. This leads you to be more nervous and will create a kind of vicious circle.

Another thing, however, is to observe the signals in the child that make you understand that she is potentially ready, but not wanting to follow them.

Perhaps you are not motivated enough or due to lack of time for work or other, the start of the phase is postponed. However, this will result as a lack of listening in the child who will continue to rely on the diaper and will have to relearn again to understand her own stimuli and to control them (probably with greater difficulty).

Furthermore, I advise you, if you undertake this phase, to do it in the most consistent and disciplined way possible.

For example, answering the child who suddenly asks us to pee when you are in the city center "Love, this time do it in the diaper" would be an attitude that can generate confusion in your child, who will not be able to distinguish when to pee herself off and when in the potty. If, on the other hand, despite the possibility that she does it in the diaper due to the distance from the bathrooms, inviting her to pee by removing the diaper will communicate to your child that you listen to her needs. This will help her to learn to control herself and stimulates her cause she will know that, as soon as possible, you will enable her to free herself.

You may think that children are not ready, but most of the time the parents are not ready to lead their children towards the big leap.

If you remain calm and in control, if you accept that like any path this too is marked by progressions and regressions, no one will get hurt. Indeed, family life will be enriched with nice anecdotes to tell during family reunions.

Outdoor "Emergencies"

In the early stages of the transition between the diaper and the potty, as we said earlier, absorbent panties will be a good help. When you are away from home and the baby is unable to pee in time, she will not dirty her clothes and she will not feel uncomfortable.

If you really can't find a public toilet, or if that isn't right for you, you can choose the quickest way, find a small plant or an isolated area in which to have your child empty her bladder. Let the boy or girl understand that this is an emergency solution, not a habit. But be careful because in some cities this "practice" is prohibited by the law and you may incur a fine.

Some parents choose to carry a potty in the car so it can be pulled out whenever needed. This is especially useful if you are traveling long distances.

There are some very interesting potty models. Some are space-saving, they fold and become flat, can be slipped into a bag or stored in the lower compartment of the stroller. They are versatile because they act as a potty with the fins mounted vertically or as a reducer with the fins arranged horizontally. They are not expensive, they are hygienic because pee and poo are collected in the supplied bags that fold in a few moments and are thrown away without leaving unpleasant odors.

Here are other suggestions to limit emergencies as much as possible:

Try to leave the house only after the baby has just used the bathroom. This will limit the need to run to the bathroom with a half-full shopping cart

The use of panties for potty training will allow the child to feel comfortable at home as well as traveling

Find out the location of the nearest toilets, wherever you go. Take a quick tour to check the status before she needs it, so that she feels comfortable when she feels the urge to use the toilet

Bring a change of clothes with you as they may always come in handy

If you are almost at the finish line of toilet training and your child is no longer wearing potty training panties, disposable sheets can act as a comfortable cover for the car seat in case of minor accidents

Public Restrooms

It's very normal for newly trained (or still-learning) children not to want to go potty in public restrooms, which appear to be unfamiliar, daunting and noisy.

One easy solution: use the toilet before you leave the house. Reduce your trips to a minimum and keep your trips quick and convenient when you go out so that, when the urge pops up again, you'll be home in time to go potty in a familiar location.

The biggest problem with public toilets is undoubtedly noise. This can be very disturbing for sensitive children.

You can reduce the noise by:

— Bringing earmuffs or headphones of children's size with you

— Avoiding toilets with plenty of doors. If there's one, look for a family restroom; this is usually a smaller space with only a toilet and sink, much like your home bathroom

— Covering the sensor on an automatic flush toilet so that it won't annoy your kids. You can use a sticky piece of paper or your hand

— Letting your child go and wait by the sink while you're flushing

— Carrying your hand towels or paper towels, so you don't have to use hand dryers

Remember to always strictly follow the sanitary rules when you are in a public bathroom.

It is also important to teach the child not to touch "everything" in public toilet. If they are old enough to stand on their own legs, this is doable, but if they are small, the game can be more difficult.

Also, children tend to hold onto the toilet seat quite automatically and, not knowing who has been in that bathroom, they could really risk getting sick (as children tend to put their fingers in their mouths). Eventually you can clean the toilet, but it is difficult to carry cleaning products around, especially during an emergency (and let's be honest, who would like to clean a toilet in a public bathroom?).

Another possibility is travel covers, which are very comfortable because they are plasticized and very wide, fantastic for those who take long trips with their children.

At the moment of use, just open them, place them on the board. When the child finishes her business, you can throw them away. Some models are equipped with adhesive strips so there is no danger of them moving. They are disposable, they are waterproof and can be found in any supermarket. They are also easier to use than toilet paper on the edge of the toilet. The toilet paper is not so hygienic for this purpose because placing it on the toilet, it could still get wet due to residues left by someone else.

Emergency Kit

Now I will list some of the items you can take with you when you are away from home:

- wet wipes

- anti-mosquito wipes, especially for the summer

- toilet paper wipes, which refresh and are biodegradable

- plasticized toilet seats

- small towel, as it may be needed to clean the baby

- patches of various sizes

- anti-redness cream

- panties

- plastic bag, for storing dirty or wet wipes or towels

- markers and paper, to entertain her especially when she is in public places and there are no children to play with.

Conclusion

There are many ways to potty train. Whatever method you use, stock up on underwear and work hard to stay positive, or at least push through it with a smile, because they're watching you. Parents, you are one of the most important figures for your children because they will take an example from you.

Ensure you use the evening to "charge the batteries" whatever way you prefer and, most of all, acknowledge that using the toilet is a big life skill and you are in this together.

Be cool, calm, and confident, and your child will follow your lead. You'll be so proud of your kid (and yourself!) when you're done.

So, I hope you will treasure my advice and wish you the best of luck!

Made in the USA
Coppell, TX
29 September 2021